IN THIS ISSUE

I0045314

PIVOT Magazine

Founder and President
Jason Miller

Editor-in-Chief
Chris O'Byrne

Design
JETLAUNCH.net

Advertising
Chris O'Byrne

Webmaster
Joel Phillips

Editor
Laura West

Cover Design
Debbie O'Byrne

Copyright © 2024 PIVOT

ISBN: 979-8-89079-108-5

LETTER FROM THE EDITOR

In this edition, we spotlight Dr. Jen Welter, an icon in the sports world and the first woman to coach in the NFL. Her story, rich with challenges and triumphs, is a compelling narrative of leadership, innovation, and resilience. I had an enlightening discussion with Dr. Welter where she shared her journey, shedding light on the essentials of navigating and excelling in environments that challenge traditional norms. Her story is a lesson in daring to venture into new territories, the power of enduring through adversity, and the art of authentic leadership.

Dr. Welter's achievements go beyond her groundbreaking role in the NFL. As an academic, speaker, author, and founder of Grrridiron Girls, she exemplifies a multidimensional approach to success. Her book *Play Big* and her other initiatives underscore her commitment to effecting societal change through sports and leadership.

This issue is a source of inspiration and insight for anyone looking to make a significant impact in their field, offering a fresh perspective on what it means to lead, persevere, and innovate.

Chris O'Byrne

FROM THE DESK OF THE PRESIDENT

JASON MILLER

Our latest issue is a treasure trove of insights and inspiration, featuring the extraordinary Dr. Jen Welter. As the first female NFL coach, Dr. Welter's journey is more than a sports story—it's a roadmap for leadership, breaking barriers, and entrepreneurship.

In a candid conversation with Chris O'Byrne, Dr. Welter unpacks the crucial lessons from her trailblazing journey. This is more than just her story; it's a blueprint for anyone looking to lead and succeed in uncharted territories.

Key Takeaways for Our Readers:

1. **Embrace New Challenges:** Dr. Welter's foray into a male-dominated field is a masterclass in exploring and conquering new frontiers. Learn how to identify and seize unconventional opportunities in your business or career.

2. **Resilience as a Tool for Success:** The obstacles and setbacks Dr. Welter faced and overcame are lessons in resilience. Discover how to build this resilience and use it for growth and success.

3. **Authentic Leadership:** Dr. Welter's approach to

leadership and respect is unique and effective. Gain insights into developing a leadership style that resonates with your authentic self, fostering trust and stronger team dynamics.

Why This Matters to You:

- **Entrepreneurs and Business Leaders:** Dr. Welter's experiences offer valuable lessons in navigating uncharted business landscapes and leading under pressure.
- **Aspiring Leaders:** Learn from Dr. Welter's innovative approaches to goal setting and leadership that defy conventional norms.
- **Sports Enthusiasts and Coaches:** Gain insights into team dynamics and motivational strategies from a pioneering figure in sports coaching.

Dr. Welter's varied roles—as a groundbreaking NFL coach, PhD holder, speaker, and author—demonstrate her multifaceted approach to success. Her book *Play Big* and her work, including founding Grrridiron Girls, underscore her commitment to societal transformation through sports and leadership.

This issue is an experience in learning from one of the most inspirational figures in sports today. Dr. Welter's journey is a compelling guide to leadership, resilience, and the entrepreneurial spirit. Join us in uncovering the powerful lessons she imparts for personal and professional growth.

MY PATH TO SUCCESS: TACKLING THE FINAL FRONTIER IN SPORTS

DR. JEN WELTER

Chris O'Byrne:

What story or event from childhood helped you develop into who you are today?

Jen Welter:

When I was a little girl, I looked at my dad and matter-of-factly said, "Daddy, it's a really good thing I was born now." When he asked why, I said, "They would have burned me at the stake."

I had just learned about Joan of Arc and how amazing she was, how she dressed in men's armor and led them into battle. Fast forward to modern-day football and the armor we wear, and here I am, coaching football as a woman. We're seeing major progress in society. Women serve, armed and ready, in different areas of the military. Women are armed for battle in their business suits and leading men onto the field of the gladiator sport, football. There was something about that moment as a little kid. I knew I could lead, and I knew I could do what the boys did and eventually lead men.

We teach kids to forget what they know. Little Jen was confident. She heard about a woman in history doing something different and impactful. She knew you could get burned at the stake for doing what guys did and fearlessly wanted to do it anyway. However, that little girl forgot that along the way. We're often told what box to fit into, that what girls should do and what boys should do are different. That fearlessness goes away; at least, it did for me. I was told girls couldn't play football. In high school, I struggled with the desire to fit in instead of stand out.

I didn't have the opportunity to play football again until I was twenty-two. It was a challenge to take on an area of society where girls and women traditionally didn't go. They call football the final frontier for women in sports. For me, that was a challenge. I played my way through this belief that if this was the final frontier—the place where women and girls were not supposed to go—that when we conquered this, we could do anything. Wasn't this the proof that women could do anything in sports? Even when I was playing, I never thought I could be a coach because

there was no one I could look at and say, "I want to be her." But that young Jen saw something different.

When I made my first football team, I promised myself that I would step up to every challenge the game put in my way. I had no idea what I was getting myself into. There was no trail to follow. I was leading from the front, which all women in football have been doing up until now because there's no established path. Doors remain closed, and barriers need to be broken.

Many people talk about having a big vision. College is an example. If your goal is to finish college, it is doable; there is a path. There is a certain number of classes you must take, boxes you must check, and things you must do. There's a relatively established timeline. Some people do it earlier. Some people take a break and return to it, but the coursework is laid out.

We know how to set goals when we start with the end game in mind. Having a Ph.D. in psychology, I taught courses on goal setting. But one day I stopped and realized none of that applied to the success that I had in my life when people were looking at the biggest things I've done because I didn't get to start with the end game in mind. People often say, "If you can see it, you can achieve it." Seeing it is the dream and that dream gives the kernel of inspiration that

inspires the work and measurable progress. But if you can't see it, the way to get to it is to keep stepping up and doing little things every day that set you up to overcome future challenges.

I lovingly say that God put blinders on my life at times, which kept my head down and humble so I didn't get distracted by the stadium lights. Too often, if you look up and look too big, you get blinded by the lights and stumble. I'm still a work in progress, but I remember that little girl who knew it. I don't know if Joan of Arc knew she would be burned at the stake, but her visions of impact were bigger than the deterrence. And that's what we hope for.

Chris O'Byrne:

What were some of the high and low points in your career?

Jen Welter:

Much of it was being told what I couldn't, shouldn't, and wouldn't do. I am a 5'2" woman, which doesn't traditionally make a good football player. I was never told I'd be one of the best football players in the world. I was the kid who was told that because of my size and build, I was too small to play tennis. Then, I was a collegiate rugby player playing prop, the front row of the scrum—not where most people would put me. I was sometimes outweighed by about 100 pounds by the best in the game. I made it to an under-twenty-three national team tryout but didn't make it. They said I was too small. Since I was so small, I almost didn't go to my football tryout when I finally got it, but I did. Taking that step was a hard one. This is a game I have loved my whole life, but I got scared like so many people do.

However, I realized that I could live with being too small. What I couldn't live with was wondering for the rest of my life what would have happened if I had gone out for that football team.

I started the football journey and stuck with it. There were bigger, faster, stronger, better football players than me, especially when I started. But the longevity is where we become great. I couldn't be discouraged because I wasn't a standout in my first year. But my second year, I was. I had the dedication to keep going. My team went through hell early in my career, and I moved to Dallas. My first team in Dallas was also tough. We had twelve players left at our last game. I played a quarter on the O-line. It was a terrible quarter and not something that ever should happen. But three days later, I tried out for the team I played with for ten years. With that team, I won four Super Bowls in five years. It was one of the greatest dynasties women's football has ever seen—the Dallas Diamonds. And that was my family.

I played my way through hard times in life, overcoming an abusive relationship, leaving, living out of my car, getting back up, doing it again, going to practice, and continuing to push because, on the football field, I could do anything, even when the rest of my life was falling apart. I also got a Ph.D. at that time and then had the opportunity to play on the first women's US national team and win a gold medal. I also went back and won a second gold medal. Those things fortify

you and make you who you are. They taught me how to be a great teammate. They taught me to love people for being different.

I'd see how someone blocked on the football field and realize that was the person I want to run with in life because, if they do it on a football field, they'll do it for you in the real world, too. They didn't always need to be in the spotlight, but those people are who you want to be with in the trenches. That's why people talk about those locker room lessons. The women I played with motivate me in every fight I take on. If I was the one who was first, I had to lead from the front with the motivation of everyone who helped me get there. Sometimes, when I'm scared and don't feel like I have it, the women I played with and all the girls who I want to see the world differently motivate me.

When I moved into the men's pro football space, it was the first head coach I played for on the Texas Revolution, Wendell Davis, who did the crazy thing of having the first female running back in men's pro football, and we're still super tight to this day. When he calls, I answer because I wouldn't be where I am today if he hadn't bet on me when everybody thought it was a terrible idea. I'd do anything possible for him. Thankfully, this is much easier because I don't have to take the hits now. I just have to tell somebody else how

to take them. It's much easier to say yes to coaching. It was Wendell Davis who refused to let me turn down my first coaching opportunity in men's pro football. He would not let me turn him down. I instinctively tried to turn him down because I hadn't seen a woman coach and couldn't see it for myself, but he drop-kicked me into success.

Additionally, Bruce Arians risked his reputation as one of the greatest football minds in the game's history by saying, "This hasn't changed in the history of the NFL." He bet on me.

Brad Childress hired me for the Atlanta Legends. Rod Woodson hired me for the Vegas Pipers. All those men had to take risks on me. There weren't women in those positions to be able to make that happen. I look at all those decisions as part of a cool legacy that I can continue to pay forward. That is the opportunity and responsibility of being first.

I didn't set out to coach football. That was never my goal. Mine was a progression from player to coach. Wendell Davis saw the way that the players of the Texas Revolution responded to me. He said, "You have to coach this football team." Initially, I said no, but his point was interesting because I had never coached before. He told me he could teach me how to coach football, but he couldn't teach the respect and the way the guys responded to

me and listened to me. He saw that as something special.

There's no one right way to get into coaching. There's a lifelong learning process to get better at coaching. It's vital to be surrounded with great people. The hardest part of being a woman in coaching men's professional sports is that we don't have the same level of locker room interconnectivity, that same easy network. For a guy who played football, every guy in the locker room with him has a football network, whether it be guys they played with in high school, college, or professionally. For women, we have the women we played with, but there are not enough women in coaching positions to be fluidly moving through the football community. Coaching is a relationship business. You have some very, very long days together. As a coach, you have to look at the value players bring from a sports and human perspective.

Chris O'Byrne:

How does someone go about earning respect?

Jen Welter:

For any person in any role, authenticity is where you earn respect because there's no one-size-fits-all leadership style. If I had tried to replicate the leadership style I saw everywhere, it would be inauthentic to me. A good example of this is communication. A former player who's now coaching and a current player stand toe to toe. They're going at it—loud voices, big stakes, big everything. They're toe to toe, chest to chest, eye to eye. It is a very different dynamic than a short woman. We might be toe to toe, but then we're probably going to be chest to belly button, and we're certainly not going to be eye to eye, which means I'm not in your face.

I can't use the same communication methodology because I can't yell loud enough for any of them to have to listen—but anyone could lean into a whisper. For me, one-on-one communication, as opposed to a call-out that might create the dynamic of confrontation, was paramount. Building relationships and one-on-one communication are tools that helped me earn trust. I focus on putting the relationship and trust at the forefront instead of the back end. If you trust me with your life and the things you value the most, it's very easy to adjust the football technique. I believe leadership should be based on empathy and understanding, not commanding and position-oriented respect.

Chris O'Byrne:

Who were some of the key female influences or mentors in your life?

Jen Welter:

Nancy Lieberman has been a great friend of mine and was probably the closest to a mentor because we had parallel journeys in different sports, which I advocate for because there's no inherent competition. For example, I will never coach a basketball team. That would be the worst decision an organization could make because basketball is not my sport. However, we were both women coaching men's teams. We often laugh and tell each other that we took the words right out of the other person's mouth. We are in different sports, but what we have in common is we love sports and breaking barriers in men's sports. I had amazing women I played with, but that's a different dynamic in terms of opening doors career-wise. Men often opened those major doors.

I've had great women around me, but they were more teammates than role models. That's one of the things I speak on the most and why I drive so hard in the way I do is because my goal is to be the woman I needed and didn't have. I didn't have women in these positions to look up to in my football career.

My mom is another amazing role model, but as an art teacher, she looks at what I do and thinks, *My daughter's an alien*. She's wonderful and warm, and I get a lot of who I am from her, but

she wasn't a model for my own career.

One of the hardest things in my life has been direct mentorship. We don't do a good job explaining there won't always be that direct person. You can find elements of inspiration, motivation, and coaching in multiple packages, but they won't always be perfectly like you.

Working in men's pro football, all my head coaches and owners were men. I had phenomenal teammates when I played in women's pro football, and I've had wonderful women friends who have helped me in business endeavors. Some incredible women have broken barriers, like Billie Jean King, but I don't have daily access to women like her. You can look from afar, but in terms of being coached through specific situations, unfortunately, that's not the case. That's something I wish I had more of.

It's not easy, and it's lonely. I don't think most people realize just how hard it is. At the same time, I'm trying to be that person for other people. Throughout my career, people would look at where I was and ask for advice. I felt like I was still trying to figure that out. I have more questions than I do answers. The only thing I know is not to quit. It's also important to realize that without direct guidance, you will look back at your footsteps and think you would never do that again if you had the choice.

Chris O'Byrne:

Can you tell me more about the Grrridiron Girls football camps?

Jen Welter:

Grrridiron Girls was the first real national movement for girls in flag football. Football was a place in the world that made me believe I could do anything. I worked on the "Keep Playing Like a Girl" campaign and authored some of their literature. Something struck my heart when I learned that half of the girls who participated in school when they were younger walked out of sports during puberty. The reason they gave was that seven out of ten girls felt like they didn't belong in sports. Seven out of ten said that society didn't support them in sports. Seven out of ten said there were insufficient visible female role models in sports. When I read that, I knew I could be the woman who put a ball in their hands and a dream in their hearts. When approaching Grrridiron Girls, I say, "We teach confidence through football and teach girls there is no game they cannot play and no field they do not belong in or on."

The goal is to take an area where girls have traditionally been told they can't do it or don't belong and show them there is no such thing as throwing or catching like a girl. You either throw the football like you've been taught, or you haven't learned yet. You either catch the ball properly, or you don't. You deserve to know diamonds are something you get when you win championship rings and you can be a great receiver.

We focus on teaching so that through a Grrridiron Girls Camp, the girls know they can step into any streetball game, family game, or school competition, have all the basic skills, and feel good about themselves. If they don't want to play, that's okay, too. But they get to try it, learn it, and make their own decisions.

Grrridiron Girls has been a real passion of mine since 2017. I'm proud to say that many of the top girls playing today came through a Grrridiron Girls Camp at one time. We partner with great organizations locally to

help drive that interest and the initial uptake of football. Then, hopefully, they'll grow with the organization and continue to play because we can't be all things to all people all the time.

Chris O'Byrne:

How many of those camps are there per year? Are they all around the country?

Jen Welter:

We've done sixty so far and can bring a camp to any city. It's all about finding great partners. With Grrridiron Girls Camps up to this point, they've been free. It is a question of funding and partnership to bring them to a community.

Chris O'Byrne:

Have you thought about what comes next after coaching? Or is coaching one of those things you plan to do for as long as possible?

Jen Welter:

I'm not sure. I love coaching, so I'll always be coaching in one capacity or another, whether on the men's or women's sides, professionally or unprofessionally. Grrridiron Girls is coaching, too, just a different level of coaching. The Olympics in 2028 will have flag football for the first time. It would be a dream to be a part of that, bringing that to girls. And it's for boys, too, but my heart will probably be on the girl's side in that. Eventually, it could also be owning a team or being part of an ownership group. I would thrive in that environment because I haven't gotten that challenge yet. So, who knows? My journey has taught me to remain open and fall in love with the process. My very simple, big goal is stepping up to the challenges the game puts in my way, but I don't know what that next challenge is yet.

Chris O'Byrne:

What are some parting words of wisdom you can share?

Jen Welter:

Tap back into that young you, that kid who fought dragons with a wooden spoon and a pot on your head and looked at the world through an imaginative lens. I tap back into that often. That's part of the reason why I do so much with kids. I have a kids' book series because I love that young self. I love that self that wasn't bound by the lessons that sometimes take away the fearlessness we had. In adulthood, we have to pay bills and have responsibilities. Adulthood can be restrictive. Don't be afraid to go back to not overthinking things, to just going after a dream, trying something different, being a little awkward, or getting ugly. When I coach in Grrridiron Girls, I tell the girls, "To get really good, you've got to be willing to get really ugly. Who's excited about getting ugly with me?" That gets them excited.

Can you imagine if we did that more as adults? If we put away the suit and tie, if we took away the image or the idea of self of what we have to be, and we just let go and were willing to get ugly again. How much fun could we have? How many things could we disrupt? In how many areas could we shake things up? That's what I challenge myself to do, to not get so limited by role and responsibility, which is very hard for me. There's a certain expectation that comes with anything I do in football, so I wrote a kid's book. Nobody expects my kid's book to be earth-shattering, but maybe it will be. There's a lot of freedom in allowing yourself to just get ugly and get young and leave the adulting to somebody else for a little bit.

Chris O'Byrne:

Where would you like people to go to learn about you and what you're doing?

Jen Welter:

I'm active on LinkedIn, so that's a great place to follow. It's Welter47, or you could just search for me. I was one of the Top Voices on LinkedIn. It's Welter47 on Instagram, and jenwelter.com is my website.

Action Steps

1. Embrace Uncharted Territories: The author's experience in venturing into male-dominated sports like football can inspire you to explore new markets or niches in your business that haven't been traditionally pursued. By stepping into unfamiliar territory and breaking conventional boundaries, you can discover untapped potential and opportunities for innovation and growth.

2. Cultivate Resilience and Persistence: The challenges and setbacks faced by the author in her career highlight the importance of resilience. Apply this lesson to your business by embracing challenges as opportunities for growth. Stay persistent in your endeavors, even when outcomes aren't immediately visible. This mindset can help you navigate through tough times and emerge stronger.

3. Foster Authentic Leadership: The author's approach to earning respect through authenticity emphasizes the value of genuine leadership in business. Implement a leadership style that is true to your personality and values. By building trust and fostering genuine connections with your team, clients, or customers, you can create a more engaged and committed workforce, leading to a more successful and sustainable business.

About the Author

Dr. Jen Welter is a groundbreaking, barrier-busting force of nature. She is a female trailblazer, a sports pioneer, PhD, passionate leader, world-renowned speaker, entrepreneur, and source of inspiration around the globe. Her relentless pursuit of individual excellence and success in challenging the status quo time and time again, fuels her current drive to help others achieve their best—in sports, health and wellness, professional pursuits, and in life.

Dr. Jen embodies the philosophy that greatness is a choice, repeatedly demonstrating this in every field she enters. Her impressive football career is marked by numerous firsts, including playing on the men's professional team, becoming the first female NFL coach, and being featured in the Madden NFL 20 video game. Her book, *Play Big: Lessons in Living Limitless from the First Woman to Coach in the NFL*, encapsulates her journey. Beyond her personal achievements, Dr. Jen is committed to societal transformation through sports. She founded Grrridiron Girls, the first national girls' flag football movement, and is recognized by President Obama as a trailblazer. Her work extends from coaching young athletes to advising C-level executives, emphasizing the power of voice and fearless conversations in driving positive change.

Dr. Jen's message of overcoming life's obstacles with grit, tenacity and limitless possibility has received worldwide acclaim, by audiences ranging from global companies and top schools to brands, nonprofits, and professional sports teams.

A CHILD WITH NO PRESENTS WHO NOW GIVES TO EVERYONE

WILL BLACK

Imagine a sweet, ten-year-old girl sitting on the steps in front of her parents, and younger siblings on Christmas morning when her parents look at her and say, "You're not getting *anything* for Christmas." Of course, she didn't believe them, but one after another, gifts came and went, and nothing was placed in front of her. Every other child received gifts while she sat quietly and meekly.

She waited.

No gift came.

Let's make it worse.

She was abused. She was molested. She knew little to no joy in a house that on that day would see every child get up with their gifts and eventually walk off while she sat there alone, neglected, and abused on this Christmas day in a whole new way. The abuse would continue.

This could be the back story of your average super villain in a comic book movie adaption. You'd think this is how the Grinch got started. Many people would (and do) use this type of start in life as a lifelong road of cold and distant anger aimed at a world that they could only imagine to be filled only with such pain.

But not for Michelle Williams who speaks openly and freely of her torment and struggles. Michelle started My Kind of Dad, a nonprofit that showers children in gifts, provides for children of incarcerated parents, and builds special moments for children that would otherwise see cold, sad days but instead gives them moments of joy with keepsakes that last a lifetime.

For Michelle, the right dad came in the form of her now-husband who stands beside her through the good and the bad. He helped her build her own family which, by the way, has often put her Christmas morning back on the steps only this time to be covered in enough gifts, packages, and kisses, to rival everything the Grinch stole from the Whos down in Whoville.

So inspired, Michelle often builds her own house into a "winter wonderland" to bring in children and have them leave awash in gifts. They visit parents in jail to find out what the children like best, their favorite colors, and often to get the parent(s) to write

a letter that the child can keep to remember.

My Kind of Dad is not about materialism, but rather fostering moments in the minds of children who still have that capacity for joy, that capacity for magic still rich in their heads. A few special such moments can be carried like a snow globe of happiness all year and all childhood long. Michelle knows that and gives richly. She has personally been to the edge and looked down, but she came back fighting. She came back loving and wants to help other children while there's still time.

If you have a business and would like to help My Kind of Dad, the link below is your portal to help children all year long.

saving.sharingthecredit.com/
MyKindofDad

FOR EVERY BUSINESS & BUDGET

Looking for a website design firm or D.I.Y. platform that can help you build a visually stunning and effective online brand? Look no further than our expert team. At Proshark, we help you build a customized website that meets your unique needs and goals and converts visitors to customers.

PROSHARK SITES

INNOVATION DESIGNED TO INSPIRE

www.proshark.com

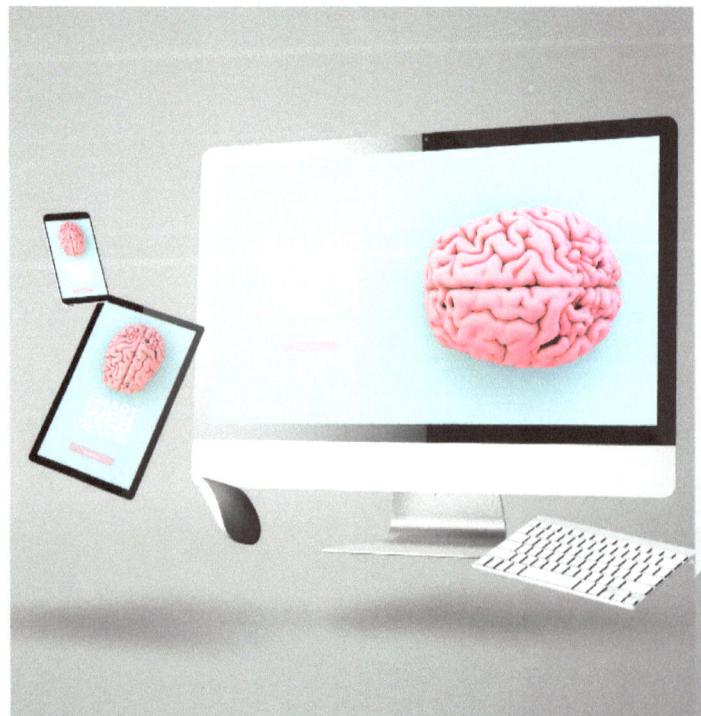

DISCOVERING AND SHARING WISDOM IN MODERN NETWORKING

BEN ALBERT

Chris O'Byrne

What is the big picture of what you do?

Ben Albert

From a broad perspective, my goal is to bridge the gap by transferring wisdom, knowledge, and lessons from those who possess them to those who seek them. Whether it involves podcast hosting, establishing genuine business connections, contributing to marketing efforts at Balbert Marketing to attract the right clients, or actively participating as a dedicated networker and networking group host, I often need wisdom. I aim to continually learn, engage others, and effectively convey lessons and stories as I navigate my journey.

It's an individualized process. I remind myself of this often with a keychain I have. It bears the inscription *There is no key*, a playful nod since it's a keychain.

I often joke about the absence of a singular key to success or fulfillment. It's not a straightforward A-to-B journey; it's not linear. Instead, it's comparable to a combination lock. Each person holds a unique and individualized combination to unlock their path.

In the quest to discover one's essence, the analogy holds true. Think about our fingerprints. Why are they taken, especially when we face challenges? It's because each of us possesses a distinct fingerprint, a unique DNA, and an exclusive essence.

There are two key steps to authentically discovering our identity. First, we must engage in the inner work. Second, we must establish our combination by surrounding ourselves with the right people, finding the right mentors, connecting with like-minded peers, and locating our sweet spot.

It's all about learning. If you have a playbook, I want to learn your playbook. Yet, I also recognize the importance of acquiring the skills to make spontaneous changes and create strategies based on who I am. It circles back to my earlier statement: There's no single key; it's akin to a combination lock.

The goal, shared by everyone, must be to discover our unique combination and essence. That's the path to achieving pretty much whatever we want. It's about what I want, what Chris wants, rather than conforming to societal expectations of what we *should* want. It's our individualized journey.

Chris O'Byrne

How do you find that uniqueness? Or if somebody wants to do it independently, how do they figure that out and unlock the combination?

Ben Albert

Our stories tell a lot about who we are. All the answers are inscribed in our past, shaped by the person we want to become.

There are two things we can do. First, let's do a past exercise. Consider people who played the role of mentors or antagonists in your life. Examine stories where you had a mentor possessing certain values and a particular skill set that you aspired to emulate. What do these stories reveal? What values and skill sets did they have? Write those stories down. Compile a list of those values because I believe they are likely reflected in your current beliefs and skills.

Do the same thing with antagonists. These are generally stories where people exhibited a deficiency in certain values— compassion, kindness, a growth mindset, or patience. You might have developed patience as a trait due to a lack of it in your interactions with your father. Reflect on these stories. What was lacking? What did you possess in abundance? What do those stories offer about the person you have evolved into today? This exercise provides background on who you are and how those moments shaped your life.

Next, observe your mentors. Examine the person six days, six weeks, six years, or sixty years ahead of you. What lessons can you extract from them to cast aside the negatives of the past, embrace the positives, and use these mentors to propel yourself forward?

I understand it's quite a lot to consider, but we can turn inward to examine our past, values, and defining characteristics and then scrutinize those individuals we aspire to emulate. How do they behave? What actions do they take? What systems and processes do they follow? This introspection allows us to chart our course, moving toward and surpassing the people who serve as our mentors.

Chris O'Byrne

How does understanding my values and identifying the values

I want to develop contribute to defining my uniqueness?

Ben Albert

I don't know if that necessarily helps you figure out your uniqueness, except that it helps establish your unique place within the tribe and community, determining the people you'll serve and the foundation of what you will build.

Therefore, if genuine compassion holds significant value for you, my assumption and wager are that you'll gravitate toward an industry that embodies compassion. If your current industry doesn't, you might sense a disconnect. This misalignment will likely push you to surround yourself with the right community of people with similar or complementary skills.

I don't know if that makes you unique because you're in a community of like-minded people, but what sets you apart are your storylines. Where did compassion play a crucial role in your life? Why are you working in this industry? Why are you excited about what you do? These narratives will be unique and magnetic to those who resonate with such stories.

When creating content, you might say the same thing that Chris, Ben, and fifty others have already said. Still, you'll be presenting it through your lens,

drawing upon your reservoir of stories and experiences.

Does this render you inherently unique? Not fundamentally. At the core, the underlying value remains consistent—a universal thread. What sets you apart is your personal touch, your storytelling style, and the uniqueness of your experiences.

Chris O'Byrne

Let's say I've gone through the process, and I understand my values, how they make me unique, and how I like to express them. How do I apply that to my business?

Ben Albert

It's huge when articulating the reasons behind your endeavors and identifying the people you want to help. It's also huge when weaving these explanations into the fabric of your narrative and personal history.

I'll give you a simple example. Throughout my childhood, I

wanted to be a basketball player. I had great shooting skills, had a wardrobe stocked with jerseys for each day of the week, and dedicated countless hours to playing. But despite my prowess, I remained at a height of 5'8", making me the shortest boy in high school.

So, guess what happened? I got pushed around. I got bullied and gave up on basketball because I felt marginalized and overwhelmed by a sense of inadequacy and a lack of belonging.

The turning point came with creating my community, Grow Getters Only. While a lot has happened since those challenging days, the experience instilled a growth mindset. Understanding the impact of feeling small, I wanted to build a community that uplifts its members, celebrates wins, and fosters the sharing of valuable information.

Because that small kid who gave up on basketball might have been the next Muggsy-Bogues; for all we know, I could have ended up being 5'8" and still made it—who knows? However, one of my life missions and core values is centered around growth and development. And that's exactly why I built a community that fosters growth, where people support each other to overcome feelings of inadequacy and uplift one another.

It serves as an example of how growth is a fundamental value for me. Facing bullying on the basketball court due to my lack of height represents a literal absence of growth in that situation. That's part of why I started Grow Getters Only—so others don't have to experience similar feelings. It's a simple example that resonates with everyone.

Chris O'Byrne

Why did you start a community?

Ben Albert

I wanted to surround myself with growth-oriented people. While this wasn't a conscious thought, it's an easy way to explain my motivation.

During a conversation with James Altucher, he introduced the concept of "plus, minus, equal." In this framework, a plus represents a mentor, and a minus is someone in a mentee role or a business context; they might be a client. An equal is a peer with whom you share referrals or information; you may not necessarily do business together, but they're a collaborator or mastermind partner.

The whole concept of Grow Getters Only was to bring in mentors—brilliant speakers I encountered through networking on the podcast—to mentor my peers. It was about fostering a dynamic where mentors could function as peers, build relationships, and do business together. This concept was at the core of why I initiated the community.

I was meeting really cool people. I feel super humble. I can't fathom why anyone would choose to spend their time with me; I'm pretty boring, Chris. Nonetheless, I wanted to introduce these great people to my community and showcase their talents. This approach provided a simple means to achieve that goal on a larger scale.

Chris O'Byrne

How did you establish relationships with people like Cal Fussman and Jordan Harbinger, ultimately making them part of your community?

Ben Albert

I prioritized my role as a student first, and there's ample content to delve into regarding this aspect alone. I dedicated a decade to learning from Jordan and James before attempting to connect with them. While I don't advocate a ten-year learning period for everyone, it's important to note that my outreach wasn't haphazard. I didn't approach people well beyond my league without prior familiarity.

My podcast journey began in 2013, and by 2014, I was actively engaged in podcast listening. In 2016, I launched a music podcast, followed by a business podcast in 2020. My approach began on a hyperlocal level, given my status as a business owner in Rochester, New York. I aimed to network with and learn from fellow local business owners, leading to the establishment of Rochester Business Connections. Over time, it underwent rebranding and evolved into Real Business Connections.

Initially, securing guests like James Alta Church and Jordan Harbinger for Rochester Business Connections was unlikely. However, I strategically built a local foundation and audience, allowing for a successful rebranding that facilitated conversations with other mentors and speakers. My podcast-listening routine involved engagement, and after each episode, I consistently reached out to hosts and guests. If I hadn't encountered a guest before, I habitually expressed my appreciation, shared three key takeaways, and extended positive messages such as subscribing, connecting, or offering support.

Over time, I began featuring fantastic guests on my podcast. The strategy I employed to find these exceptional individuals involved being a diligent consumer. Instead of selecting guests from a predetermined list or relying on guesswork, I immersed myself in podcasts featuring potential guests. Upon discovering someone remarkable, like Chris, for example, I invited them to join my podcast. This helped me cultivate a notable guest list, progressing from a solid roster to what I'll humorously refer to as a "C-list."

As I tried to attract bigger guests, I adopted a name-dropping method. Leveraging connections with previous podcast guests, I initiated outreach to individuals of greater renown. For instance, if I knew Hala Taha was connected to Alex San Filippo and Jordan Harbinger, I would reach out to Hala, expressing admiration for her work and highlighting specific insights gained from her. I'd then mention that I've had Jordan and Alex on my podcast, suggesting she'd be a good fit for my audience.

Rather than embarking on widespread outreach from day one, I built a local community before expanding to a national audience. Throughout this process, I prioritized featuring value-driven guests. To further enhance my guest selection, I actively sought nominations from my current guests who might be a good fit for the podcast.

In the long run, I incorporated name-dropping as a strategic element in my outreach efforts. For example, mentioning a prominent figure like Mark Bodin, who has a huge YouTube following, served as social proof.

Before making such references, I took the precaution of verifying connections on platforms like LinkedIn and Instagram, ensuring the assumed familiarity between individuals was accurate.

In reflection, I've come to appreciate that social proof plays a pivotal role in opening doors for me. While I may not boast conventional attractiveness—I have a "face for radio"—I believe the consistent growth, promotion, and audience-building efforts I dedicate to my show contribute quite a bit to its success.

Chris O'Byrne

I'm currently interested in the thought process that fueled your growth. It seems there was a progression from a hyperlocal focus to expansion. Was there a deliberate strategy guiding this evolution, or did it primarily involve seizing opportunities? Could you share more about the mindset you maintained during this period?

Ben Albert

It was a reactionary move driven by ego. Take Jordan Harbinger; I'd be honored to have him on my show, but that would never materialize with a locally based podcast. It's just not feasible.

Returning to our initial point, the essence lies in channeling wisdom from those who

have it to those who seek it. I fall into the latter category, craving knowledge from these people. The podcast emerged as a platform to accelerate and amplify the dissemination of such knowledge. Unfortunately, Rochester Business Connections couldn't attract those notable figures to speak with me.

Thus, I rebranded out of sheer ego-driven motivation to learn from them. Although I acknowledged the potential to share acquired knowledge, it was primarily driven by my quest. Ironically, in terms of business and entrepreneurship, sticking with Rochester Business Connections would make me more income. The proximity, in-person interactions, and coffee chats in my hometown create a higher probability of converting local business owners and clients than a large international podcast.

Maintaining a hyperlocal focus would have been the most prudent business decision—to become the go-to Rochester marketer. Rochester, New York, boasts a substantial population, presenting lucrative opportunities. However, I didn't care about the money because of my ego and love of learning. I want to be big in Rochester. However, with my passion for learning and a disregard for financial gains, I prioritized broadening my horizons. I wanted to learn from people like

Chris, James, Jordan, and Amber Leago, a prospect that seemed unattainable with the original branding. Hence, the decision to rebrand was driven by a desire to make such connections possible.

Chris O'Byrne

I appreciate the sincerity of that statement. I think that 99 percent of the people reading this have gone through or are currently going through that same process. They engage in their activities, often in a reactive manner, seizing opportunities as they arise. This behavior is partly fueled by a level of business acumen, helping them see those opportunities and move forward accordingly. What is your vision for expanding the community?

Ben Albert

I have an event scheduled for tonight, the same day as this interview, where I'll announce something new. So, it's an interesting time to ask me that because I can't divulge the details for another four hours.

Yet, it goes back to what we've already discussed—gaining wisdom from those who have it and sharing it with those in need. It involves finding our combination by learning and networking with brilliant people. While Grow Getters is the only community I've built within Real Business Connections, the podcast is just a starting point.

I'm announcing it all tonight, introducing something private and exclusive. The existing free content will remain accessible, and I plan to continue offering free options. Then, I'll introduce private options for a more in-depth collaborative experience.

I don't plan on making this a billion-dollar project, but rather to help one business owner at a time. By doing so, we can contribute to a more robust and improved business landscape.

Chris O'Byrne

I know you're speaking at the Traffic and Conversion Summit this month. Could you share how your relationship with the people running the summit and your relationship with Digital Marketer developed and why you developed that?

Ben Albert

Mark de Gras is the president of Digital Marketer. I had the pleasure of meeting Dustin Reichman, a guest on Digital Marketer, who specializes in teaching podcast guesting. Dustin introduced me to Mark, and subsequently, I had the opportunity to be a guest on their podcast. Mark and I hit it off.

You're good at this, and your active presence on LinkedIn speaks volumes. My approach goes beyond a mere conversation; I don't treat this as press for me. Instead, I am committed to continuous learning and building lasting relationships.

I continue to keep in touch with Mark, whether it's through direct messages, sharing memes, or just goofing off. Mark even spoke at one of my Grow Getters events, beginning our evolving relationship. Digitalmarketer. com used to host the Traffic and Conversion Summit in Las Vegas, featuring keynote speakers like Richard Branson and Damon John. Although a different company now oversees the event, Digital Marketer is consulting on it this year.

Mark reached out, cautioning that there were no guarantees as he was not overseeing the event. However, he encouraged me to submit a speaker application for the summit, assuring me he would put in a good word for me. This proposition, shared during a faculty meeting, reached many, but not everyone got in. I got lucky. I feel like I was born lucky because I don't know why I got in. Thankfully, I was among the fortunate few.

Feeling fortunate, I approached the application with an interesting topic title, pitching it in a way that stood out from the norm. My innovative speech earned the green light, paving the way for my participation in the summit.

The key takeaway is the significance of cultivating relationships, from podcast guesting to hosting events and maintaining consistent communication. Mark's endorsement played an important role, leading me to the opportunity to speak alongside Richard Branson. It's not about skipping the line but leveraging incremental opportunities and relationships to reach new heights.

They're selling VIP packages that are ten times the cost of a typical ticket and include a meet-and-greet. I don't know if my speaker ticket grants me access to those same rooms. I wouldn't be upset if it didn't. But I'll be honest, I haven't even thought about this, Chris. I'll probably reach out to Richard's and Damon's teams, thank them for speaking at the event, inform them of my role as a speaker, and extend an invitation for them to be on the podcast.

I plan to wait until after the event to make an offer to say, "I saw you speak, and I spoke as well." While we discuss networking, it's about adding value, making more deposits, and approaching outreach with mindfulness and strategy. It's about understanding that you're reaching out to another human being and having enough insight into human psychology and behavior to do so strategically, kindly, and compassionately to achieve the desired results.

Chris O'Byrne

How are you going to prepare for that talk? What is the reasoning behind your preparation?

Ben Albert

I'll feel embarrassed if I fail. Ego is a huge driver in most of our lives, and I'm no exception. While I don't have a solution for overcoming the ego, the thought of disappointing myself in front of an audience makes me nauseous.

And maybe that's ego-based, but the idea of having an opportunity and not performing well is distressing to me. The thought of having someone in the audience who needs the message I have to share, yet I'm underprepared, and the presentation turns into a chaotic mess, is something I find intolerable.

Honestly, my preparation revolves around determining what I'll say, understanding the direction I want to take, planning the slides, and cultivating the confidence and mindset that I am here to serve and there to deliver. If I fall short in front of the audience, I'll feel terrible; it's a missed opportunity. That's the candid answer for you.

Chris O'Byrne

Can you share what you will discuss and why you chose that topic?

Ben Albert

It's utilizing podcasting as a gold mine for social proof. Podcasting serves as a compelling case study, with very simple examples, as discussed earlier, demonstrating its effectiveness in reaching an audience of marketers. Here's a valuable tip: One of the ways I consistently gather reviews and testimonials is by requesting them at the moment during interactions.

Every day, business professionals have conversations where they share success stories, like fixing a broken system in someone's business. As an operations consultant, I've witnessed a 40 percent increase in revenue from quarter one to quarter three after resolving such issues. During these discussions, everyone is enthusiastic and excited to continue working together.

However, a common mistake occurs after the call, often hours, weeks, or months later. Rather than waiting, I advocate asking for reviews during the Zoom meeting, where you can click record and capture the endorsement immediately.

I joke all the time about the analogy of dating—the optimal time for a kiss isn't at the end of the night when both parties are inebriated and parting ways. Instead, it's an emotional high point when the energy is elevated, rapport is strong, and both individuals thoroughly enjoy their time together. Similarly, many of us delay seeking assistance, asking for reviews, or requesting testimonials until it's too late.

While podcasting is a central focus of this discussion, the key emphasis lies in developing a systematic approach to gathering reviews and testimonials from people who have benefited from your services. Also, it delves into the strategic utilization of these endorsements to bolster the social proof of your brand and business. This, in turn, amplifies your message, allowing it to reach a wider audience.

Chris O'Byrne

What kinds of questions should people ask to pull out the best testimonial?

Ben Albert

That's a good question. It could get a little awkward if it takes on too much of an interview-style approach when asked on the spot. Generally, I don't follow a script, but I express my gratitude by saying, "Chris, you brought so much value today. I appreciate you. Feel free to decline if you're not comfortable. This is a no-pressure situation. However, I'm trying to get more testimonials and reviews for the podcast to promote this episode and expand the show's reach and impact to more people, just like the listener we talked about before our conversation today. Would you be open to leaving a testimonial?"

People often wonder about the process and ask, "How do I do it?" My response is often, "We can do it right now. The recording is already in progress."

In a more structured dialogue scenario, where someone's willing to sit down and answer a few questions, the key is to inquire strategically. Questions should revolve around their situation before utilizing the service, encompassing both logical and emotional aspects, with a preference for the latter.

For example, one might share, "I had just been let go from my job, with zero dollars to my name, and I was seeking a mentor to help me start my business."

Now, the focus shifts to the process of collaboration. "Then I worked with Chris" leads to inquiries about what the collaboration entailed—the steps taken, such as A, B, C, and D.

Finally, exploring the solutions brought forth by Chris for their business becomes crucial. It's about the solution Chris brought your business. This comprehensive approach captures the collaboration's emotional journey and practical aspects.

Most people tend to approach this logically. They might express, "I began from scratch, and now, within just six months of collaborating with Chris, I'm generating $10,000 in monthly revenue."

However, based on my research, I like to probe them because emotions tend to have a more compelling impact than logic. We often discuss the logical aspects.

Then, you ask, "With an additional $10,000 per month in your business, how has this personally affected you?" The responses often reveal personal milestones, such as planning a proposal, affording a ring, sending a child to college, or alleviating mortgage stress.

Transitioning from their initial logical standpoint to the emotional journey encapsulates the depth of the testimonial, highlighting the impact of the process, system, and collaborative structure.

Concluding with inquiries that touch on logic and emotion—how this transformation has affected their business and personal life—ensures a robust testimonial every single time.

While I don't recommend going through this process spontaneously, I encourage organizing a testimonial day. Obtaining pre-approval for video reviews and scheduling a concentrated block of time, such as a three-hour Zoom session, can efficiently capture multiple testimonials in one go.

A valuable testimonial day tip is having someone other than yourself pose the questions. Whether it's a team member or a friend, their unbiased approach reduces any awkwardness. When the testimonial is for Chris from Ben, having a third party unfamiliar with the situation facilitates an authentic and comfortable interaction, allowing Chris or Ben the opportunity to answer.

Chris O'Byrne

What key takeaways do you want the audience to get from your talk?

Ben Albert

The key takeaways are consistent with what I've already said today: Success isn't found in a single key but in a combination of factors. Initiating conversations with brilliant people, be it via a podcast or a networking event, is vital. Learn from them, absorb their wisdom, and let it shape your business.

As you transform your business and refine your approach, seize opportunities where you've delivered value to request reviews. Be shameless with it. Because at the end of the day, 98 percent of people trust testimonials from strangers more than statements from the business owner.

So, stop talking about yourself. I feel nauseous after talking about myself in this interview, Chris, and about a talk that's not fully developed yet.

Surround yourself with the right people, consistently add value, and ensure you contribute more than you withdraw in a relationship because relationships will lead to something bigger. Once you've embarked on a noteworthy journey, document the experience through a podcast, a photo, a social media post, or discussing the opportunity. Request reviews to create a repository of experiences, building leverage through each success. Over time, these accumulated wins will propel you toward your desired destination.

Chris O'Byrne

How did you evolve from what you were doing before into running your marketing agency?

Ben Albert

You asked how I evolved, which is a good way to describe because we're always evolving. It's a constant evolution in our journey.

Behind the scenes, I was a podcast addict, reading personal growth literature, engaged in sales, and eventually became a sales executive for a corporate firm. I didn't always align with the established methods; instead, I developed my methodologies and sought guidance from mentors while employed in the corporate world. Thus, my background encompassed podcasting, personal growth, sales, marketing, and self-development within a corporate role.

Then, COVID hit, and I was let go. Suddenly, income, the book of business, and all momentum were completely stripped from me. I was in a dark place, but the previously mentioned elements remained integral to who I was.

People talk about saving for a rainy day in financial terms, overlooking the possibility of saving skill sets, mindset, communication skills, and experiences. Relationships, too, can be reserved for a rainy day. I always advocate for "digging the well" beforehand, a concept I adopted from Jordan Harbinger. Digging the well before you're thirsty ensures you have a well when the need arises. The best time to search for more wells or water sources is when your well is full. Waiting until your well runs dry is not advisable; you want to have multiple water sources in advance.

Returning to my story, when I was let go, I was in a dark place, but I began to systematically accumulate experiences day by day. Transitioning from a music podcast to a business-focused one, leveraging my marketing expertise from the corporate world to start a small marketing business, and utilizing my understanding of social media to build a personal brand on platforms like LinkedIn were all part of this journey. I embraced podcasting as a passion and networking tool.

I didn't do anything that exciting or different from the average Joe. I just leaned into my unique combination of experiences. Through this, I established a strong foundation that eventually replaced the void left by my previous situation.

Once again, you mentioned it in terms of evolution—a constant process of adaptation and growth. If you find yourself plateauing or heading downward, that's a negative sign. I believe our lives should be characterized by constant evolution and personal growth.

Chris O'Byrne

How did you figure out how to start a business?

Ben Albert

Google, mostly. I told my buddy I was starting a business and naming it Balbert Marketing. His response was, "Nobody even calls you Balbert!" My brother was Dan Albert. I just made up Balbert on the spot

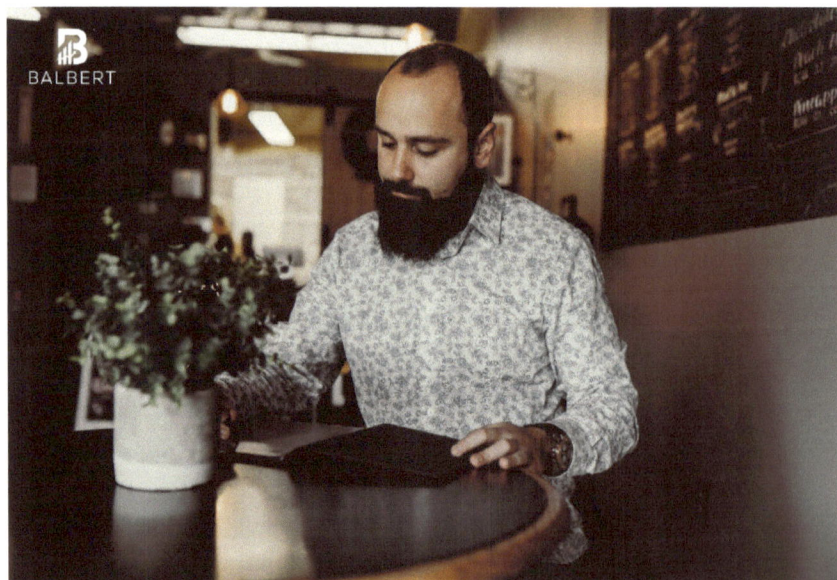

because I thought I needed an LLC to start a business. Little did I know, I could have just started freelancing from day one without the LLC. But I didn't know any of this stuff. It all connects back, like an infinity loop.

It circles back to what we already talked about. I started talking with business owners in Rochester, New York, as they knew things I didn't. Whether it was understanding accounting, CRMs, leadership, scaling, or virtual assistants, it didn't matter if someone was a realtor, a CPA, a leadership coach, or a salesperson; everyone I encountered had insights into aspects of business that I needed.

While I had a decent grasp of podcasting, marketing, and sales, I knew I had much to learn. I brought in people to instruct me in areas where I was weaker. Admittedly, my QuickBooks may not be as polished as it could be, and there are areas where I'm not as proficient as others. Nevertheless, I believe I'm strong enough to run a business, and I'm learning as I go. It's been three years.

Chris O'Byrne

What are some of those valuable lessons that you learned along the way?

Ben Albert

It's great because we've seamlessly integrated them into the discussion thus far. But a big aspect is stacking wins daily and holding yourself accountable to achieve wins each day.

I have a short to-do list every morning, and they're non-negotiables. They may seem trivial and small. For example, I participated in a podcast with Chris, invited five speakers to address my mastermind group, worked on my podcast, and fulfilled client orders. I write down these non-negotiables, and I get them done. I miss one occasionally, but I still secure far more wins than losses.

The next day, I create a new list and accomplish those tasks, accumulating even more wins. While aiming for a perfect score, I consistently achieve a high number of wins compared to losses. I firmly believe that confidence stems from the memories of winning. I can develop my inquisitive self and remain a perpetual student by continuously winning each day, staying curious, and learning. This allows me to lead by educating and helping my clients and colleagues. If I accomplish both aspects every day, I will win the day.

Hold yourself accountable. Even if it's the smallest to-do list, hold yourself accountable to ensure

a victory daily. Find your DNA code combination. Mine was marketing, sales, podcasting, and LinkedIn. Those are the things I'm best at. Focus on what you're exceptionally good at.

Another vital point we discussed is finding your niche and community. I started with Rochester, New York, business owners, but you can do this based on location, industry, a specific hobby, or even a shared value set. Also, find people whose values run parallel with yours.

I didn't have a solid grasp of this when I started three years ago. I've noticed that the more I say things with certainty and the more I express my thoughts, the more I disagree with my past self six months later. I'm in a constant state of learning and evolving. The purpose is to describe what I've learned and am going through. It's not about prescribing a singular approach; I won't assert that my way is the only way. Instead, I'm simply detailing what I've learned so far. Give it a couple of years, and I might find myself debating with my present perspective.

Chris O'Byrne

Have you successfully utilized your relationships, say from your community, podcast, or elsewhere, to support your marketing business? Has this proven to be a valuable source of lead generation for you?

Ben Albert

It's not the direct purpose of it, but I like to give people a client-like experience and an incredible experience no matter what. I encounter failures all the time, but it's an ongoing effort. I intend to exceed expectations whenever I find myself in a professional setting. Overdelivering is a priority for me, irrespective of whether the person is a client, prospect, friend, or someone I just met.

Whether they become clients, prospects, or friends, this approach establishes a perception of your business persona. They recognize your punctuality, care, and commitment to adding value by regularly overdelivering. Frequently, those people encountered in podcast conversations or random calls later become referral partners because your positive imprint remains in their minds.

So yes, such benefits accrue, but it's not a straightforward equation where fifty podcasts yield forty-eight leads. It's way more nuanced than that. I'd like to revisit your earlier point about reading books. I have no problem with that. While I could instruct someone on rapidly scaling their business, it prompts the question: Will that lead to genuine happiness? The person allocating twenty hours a week to surfing and twenty-five to their business might not scale as quickly as those working seventy hours on their business.

I'm not here to judge either scenario, but there's a distinct possibility that the twenty-hour-a-week surfer is just as content and fulfilled, even with a lower income, compared to the seventy-hour-a-week grinder. It's about understanding what works best for you and leaning into that. There isn't a universal right or wrong. You mentioned reading, and I spend hours a week immersed in books. While hiring a consultant might be more efficient, I enjoy the process of reading. I also appreciate the content on platforms like YouTube.

Chris O'Byrne

What is the grand vision of where Ben Albert is going?

Ben Albert

These are profound questions that carry significant weight. My ultimate aim is simple: to help someone every single day. I'd love to influence a million careers, one conversation at a time, and impact a million lives. I have buddies with even grander ambitions, targeting a billion, showcasing a level of ambition that surpasses mine. But I'm very confident I can do a million and impact lives.

The key word here is "actually." Consider this: If I were to undergo a transformation, showcasing a before-and-after journey of weight loss and getting a ton of likes, it might motivate someone momentarily. Yet, I question whether it would make a lasting difference in their lives or careers.

My focus is on moving the needle in a million people's lives. Just imagine the ripple effect and positive change we could collectively instigate by subtly shifting aspects of people's lives. I think this approach would enhance the overall business landscape and contribute to making the world a better place. So, let's impact a million lives. That's the goal.

Action Steps

1. **Engage in Self-Reflection and Story Analysis**: The author emphasizes the importance of understanding your own values and experiences. Reflect on your

past, particularly focusing on mentors and antagonists, and analyze how these relationships have shaped your values and skills. This introspective process can help you better understand your unique strengths and areas for growth, which can be leveraged to enhance your business strategies and decision-making.

2. **Build and Leverage Relationships**: The author highlights the significance of building relationships with mentors, peers, and potential clients. Actively seek to connect with individuals who can provide wisdom and guidance, and don't hesitate to reach out to those who inspire you. These connections can offer valuable insights, expand your network, and potentially lead to collaborative opportunities that can drive business growth.

3. **Embrace Continuous Learning and Adaptation**: The author's journey underscores the importance of being a lifelong learner and being open to evolution. Stay curious and committed to learning, whether through podcasts, books, or direct interactions with others in your field. This mindset will not only keep you updated with the latest trends and skills in your industry but also allow you to adapt and innovate in your business practices, keeping you ahead of the curve.

About the Author

Ben Albert is the owner of Balbert Marketing LLC. He is also the curator of The "Real Business Connections Network," where he hosts five podcasts. Ben is on a mission to actually move the needle on one million lives, one conversation at a time. Learn more at balbertmarketing.com.

LEADING WITH ADAPTABILITY IN BUSINESS

ALEX SNIDER

Chris O'Byrne

Can you share a significant story or experience that has played a crucial role in shaping the person you are today?

Alex Snider

That's a great question. Reflecting on my past, being an athlete growing up enhanced my strategic understanding and in-the-moment analytical skills. In equestrian, analyzing courses, measuring angles, and strategizing risks were crucial. In the heat of competition, adapting strategies based on performance and understanding event point systems became second nature.

During my twenty years in rugby, similar strategic thinking was key—knowing team strengths, studying opponents, and ensuring everyone understood their role. Whether in the ring or on the rugby field, the ability to adapt strategies on the fly and exploit opportunities has significantly shaped who I am today.

Looking back, I developed a unique way of thinking despite my quiet and shy nature that often left me feeling like I didn't quite fit in. I discovered that effective leadership doesn't always require being outspoken; instead, it involves ensuring everyone understands their roles. By caring for newcomers and making sure they feel comfortable, I realized that true leadership is about facilitating the success of the team—a concept aligning with servant leadership. In this approach, team success is personal success, and energy is invested in making sure everyone is well-informed and capable. Growing up in sports taught me strategy, honed my analytical capability, and shaped me into a servant leader; a recognized and valuable leadership style.

Chris O'Byrne

Take me on a journey from graduating high school to where you are now.

Alex Snider

Much of what I just discussed lays the foundation for my journey as I cultivated resourcefulness, a trait that unknowingly prepared me for entrepreneurship. My athletic aspirations for Team Canada were abruptly cut short due to family circumstances. This sudden shift from planning an athletic career to uncertainty about the future led me to reevaluate my path. Growing up in Canada, my parents instilled the importance of academic excellence, even if as a backup plan to my athletic aspirations. With the grades in place but unsure of my direction, I opted to complete a degree at McGill University, a globally recognized institution, in three years while simultaneously working, driven by the desire for a strong international brand and the opportunity to explore diverse possibilities.

I navigated through my university years efficiently because I just wanted to get through it. It was during this time that I was diagnosed with an autoimmune disorder. Despite not harboring fond memories of my academic journey, viewing it merely as a means to an end, I graduated with a strong GPA but without a clear path. Armed with my degree, I engaged in various endeavors, from traditional bartending to working in construction. In this unique mix, I'd transition from a construction site to tending a bar in a hip-hop club on the same day.

Continuing my quest to discover my professional calling, I explored accounting and project management roles. A twist of fate led me to assist a team of surgeons, initially intended as a short-term commitment, while I explored other opportunities. However, this evolved into a more significant opportunity as I became involved in their expansion and succession planning, transitioning into a role that required a marketing professional's expertise.

I carved out a niche with a team of oral and maxillofacial surgeons. Engaging in extensive self-teaching, I enrolled in night courses in marketing and attended conferences to immerse myself in the field. I developed analytics and metrics to quantify and track the business objectives. Ironically, I contemplated becoming an accountant during this exploration due to my affinity for numbers. I was playfully discouraged, with people noting that my personality might be too vibrant for such a role despite still leaning toward the quieter side.

Eventually, I stumbled upon strategy, business, and consulting, realizing my knack for numbers and deep interest in understanding human thinking. With an undergraduate major in psychology and a couple of arts and education minors, I questioned how these elements could align. This contemplation led me to pursue an MBA. I applied, successfully tackled the GMAT, and was thrilled to secure a spot in my program of choice, which was undergoing a fascinating shift toward a more practically applicable, less-siloed business approach.

I initially applied only to McGill at that time. From a resource standpoint, I wasn't in a position to relocate, and Montreal's relatively low cost of living aligned well with my circumstances. Despite receiving intriguing offers from other schools after my GMAT, I pursued admission to McGill because I was genuinely passionate about the program, drawn to its innovative, pragmatic approach to business, especially since I lacked a business degree. It seemed like a perfect fit for me.

Despite considering options for the next year in case I didn't secure admission, my determination prevailed.

I had graduated from high school and completed my undergraduate studies at a young age. Even though I had only the three-year minimum management experience required, I was fortunate to have strong letters of recommendation and I'd achieved impressive GMAT scores. However, I distinctly remember thinking that my chances of acceptance were slim.

During the interview, I had a great conversation with the interviewer, who, as it turned out, had a partner playing for the Springboks, South Africa's professional rugby team. This common interest provided us with plenty to bond over. Against my expectations, I was accepted into the program, becoming the youngest participant. I was apprehensive about my age being discovered. I found myself among individuals with over ten years of experience, much older than me, and with notable backgrounds, including working for the World Bank and the IMF. It had a 50 percent international composition, and I found myself alongside NASA alumni and lawyers fluent in five languages. Simultaneously, a housing crisis unfolded, leading to a hiring freeze with no internships or job opportunities. It was a challenging time.

Embarking on this new academic journey meant stepping away from work for the first time since I was twelve years old. I wholeheartedly dedicated myself to engaging in every aspect— extracurriculars, leadership roles, and academic pursuits. I served as the vice president 'internal' for the MBA Student Association, co-president of the Marketing Club, and the rugby team captain. Every waking hour was spent at school, participating in events, collaborating with the administration on changes, and contributing to the incoming class's orientation. I was determined to extract the maximum value from those two years of participating in internships, exchanges, and any opportunity that came my way. During this time, I unexpectedly embarked on an exchange program at the National University of Singapore, a decision I hadn't initially planned. The experience was extraordinary.

One of my most vivid memories and life lessons is visiting the career services office to discuss my career goals. Although I initially mentioned an interest in marketing consulting when applying, deep down, I knew I wanted to pursue strategy consulting. During our conversation, the career services advisor candidly pointed out that I was aiming for one of the two most challenging industries—investment banking and strategy consulting. They suggested considering a robust plan B, which should have been disheartening but was invaluable advice in retrospect as it galvanized me to achieve my dream against the odds.

I fully committed myself to the program, driven by sheer determination. Despite being the youngest and having limited experience without a traditional business background, I worked tirelessly and finished in the top 5 percent of my program.

Toward the end of the program, in the third semester before heading to Singapore, I received multiple job offers in my dream field, marking a significant stroke of fortune. Returning from

Singapore, I had a job waiting for me in Montreal.

I remember my first day I met my clients before meeting my own team! For the initial eight months, I immersed myself onsite with clients, gaining valuable experience of the energy and natural resource industry, primarily in Eastern Canada. About a year after joining, KPMG acquired the company I was working for, adding a layer of complexity to the situation. While the boutique French company had a close-knit community of nonconformists, I had envisioned expanding the company's reach when I joined SECOR, discussing the possibility of opening more offices. With Paris and New York already established but no new offices on the horizon, I considered the acquisition an opportunity to pursue my original plan, so I decided to stay and see how things unfolded.

Over time, I expanded operations, working extensively in western Canada and even taking on projects in Africa. This experience brought me closer to the UK team, leading to a recruitment offer for a position in London. During my three to four years there, I focused on strategy operational optimization, transitioned to the mergers and acquisitions team, and played a significant role in divestments worldwide. Additionally, I contributed to strengthening the internal

industry expertise, leveraging my industry knowledge to facilitate growth.

As circumstances evolved, corporate transfers became a part of my journey, promoting a yearlong reflection on my career path.

I got to the point where my workload reached 144 percent utilization, increasingly larger projects and internal initiatives on top of those. Despite the growing scale and responsibility, I lacked the initial excitement and fulfillment I experienced when I entered the consulting field. Consulting initially felt like the right fit during my MBA—a place where I discovered communities of like-minded individuals, all driven and dedicated. The collaborative and hardworking environment was invigorating, especially when working on impactful projects that made a difference.

I had initially opted for a focus on energy and natural resources, influenced by reflections on the financial crisis during my master's degree. Understanding the consequences of disrupting the financial systems, I recognized the tendency to overlook or negatively stereotype the energy and natural resources sector. While acknowledging its flaws, I understood these industries as essential commodities. The challenge lay in navigating a business model where extracting phones. Extractive industries are a reality. We can't simply label them as "bad" and reject them outright.

As I reflect, I realize I may have reached a point of burnout. However, I wasn't fully aware of my discontent at that time. Even though I had this great life that I had diligently built, earning praise and recognition from others, I felt an unexpected sense of unhappiness. I struggled with ingratitude and frustration, questioning why I wasn't as content as I should have been. Even as opportunities arose, steering me toward a partner track and acknowledging my unconventional approach, I found myself uninterested in these paths. I couldn't pinpoint exactly why, but it didn't align with my sense of well-being and purpose.

In response to this internal turmoil, I took action. I decided to bring some objective perspective and structure by hiring my first coach who I very serendipitously met at an event called something like Quit Your Job, Follow Your Dreams, that I attended alone because no one wanted to go with me. She was a speaker at the event, was transitioning from the military to pursue an entirely different career. We worked together, and I became one of her first clients. Our connection persisted, and we even lived together in Bali years later; life has been incredibly serendipitous. I outlined my

something didn't guarantee a predictable market value, often under unconventional working conditions.

I believed companies struggled to focus on being responsible global actors without establishing sustainable, reliable operations and a solid grip on their processes. This perspective intrigued me, as the reality is that industries like extractive ones play a critical role in producing everyday items such as toothpaste, roads, and cell objectives for leaving my job. I deliberately chose not to secure a new job immediately, opting for a budget-driven approach instead of a strict timeline. The longer I could stretch my budget, the more time I had to find a fulfilling position.

My guiding principles during this period were to feel connected, inspired, and healthy. Upon leaving the MBA, I felt the world was full of possibilities. I sought to recapture those feelings in my decisions. I engaged in house and pet sitting in various locations, providing structure and cost-free accommodations. Additionally, I dedicated time to volunteering and served on the boards of a couple of companies, and spending meaningful moments being present with people in my life.

Eventually, I invested more time in one company, contributing to strategic planning and some unique client projects. The founder, Charles, and I worked increasingly closely and eventually concluded that it presented a fantastic opportunity for me to become a partner, assisting in the organization's maturation, revitalizing its growth trajectory, and ensuring sustainability and profitability. Simultaneously, we identified a promising product opportunity that led us to co-found another startup.

When leaving KPMG, I adopted a nomadic lifestyle, selling all my possessions and living out of a suitcase. While the companies were based in Toronto, I continued to move in and out of the city, maintaining a nomadic lifestyle for about four years.

During this time, we fostered the growth of PATIO, the agency we had structured, and explored funding avenues for Scanna, the product-oriented company. The journey was exhilarating, and around late 2019, about a year after solidifying our partnership,

we conducted strategic planning for PATIO. We envisioned the next phase of maturation and growth.

Throughout the planning workshops, my business partner candidly expressed concerns about enduring another round of bootstrapped growth. Having been fully bootstrapped for about five years, exploring other options was discussed. I presented the alternative of becoming part of a larger ecosystem, outlining various ways to achieve that goal. Understanding the challenges we anticipated bootstrapping to achieve the next set of growth objectives, my partner agreed to explore joint venture or acquisition possibilities.

Around the same time, the cannabis industry, which our tech product company Scanna served, was booming in Canada. As we thought about potential partners and investors, we realized that the ones on our radar weren't the strategic allies we sought. Anticipating increased complexities, we made the wise decision to place that on hold and reevaluate our options, a decision we are thankful for in hindsight.

At that point, we shelved Scanna and directed our focus exclusively toward advancing PATIO. I was frequently in and out of Toronto during this period, even en route to Indonesia, when we had some compelling discussions. We identified potential acquirers, and recognizing the momentum, I flew back on March 13, 2020, to actively participate in the acquisition process. However, the deal faced an unforeseen hurdle as the borders closed the next day due to the onset of the COVID-19 pandemic.

Three weeks later, the deal unraveled because the potential buyer had to lay off half of their employees. Though it wasn't prudent for them, acquiring at that time didn't project a positive image. Our situation was also heavily impacted. Leading up to the transaction, we lost a couple of key team members who weren't replaced in anticipation of the impending deal. Moreover, several of our clients were massively affected, including a couple in the cannabis industry who had faced scandals just before the onset of COVID.

Suddenly, we transitioned from being on the brink of selling the company to grappling with uncertainty about its survival. Faced with these challenges, we decided to go all in. I dedicating myself entirely to the company and in response to the shifting landscape, I became well-versed in various aspects, including government subsidies and navigating the complexities of the COVID-19 pandemic. Unpacking my suitcases, I realized I wasn't going anywhere anytime soon.

We embraced the PATIO ethos of thriving in disruption to a whole new level. Our goal had always been to assist our clients in navigating and prospering amidst tumultuous times and evolving technology. Within our organization, we conscientiously incorporated antifragile thinking. Seizing the opportunity presented by a surplus of highly skilled individuals in the job market, we utilized subsidies to facilitate their onboarding. We communicated a shared vision, acknowledging openly that current compensation levels were below market standards, with a commitment to reassess salaries quarterly. Additionally, we harnessed the flexibility of our technological capabilities to make them highly relevant to the evolving context.

Long story short, we achieved a threefold growth within ten months and then sold the company. It was a year that no one would ever get back, and the intense experience likely took a toll on the health and well-being of many, myself included. Amidst the professional upheaval, I also underwent several relocations within the country, all while supporting people in my personal life. Despite the taxing nature of this period, we successfully concluded the deal with a lucrative exit in April 2021, and I transitioned to a vice president role in the acquiring company.

This juncture marked the beginning of a challenging integration phase spanning about nine months. I started my current company during this time—a venture I had long aspired to pursue. Fortunately, my business partner provided unwavering support, recognizing my innate ability to assist fellow founders. On the weekends, I collaborated with various entrepreneurs, and their consistent feedback was that our interactions left them feeling more confident and informed. Seeing the value I brought to others, I decided to leverage my experience tailoring my corporate expertise for startup environments, to assist founders in building stronger companies, teams, and leadership. It became evident that this path allowed me to multiply my impact significantly.

Even as I continued my role as vice president, I began, almost serendipitously, to pursue this new direction. I decided to part ways with the acquiring company by December of that year transitioning full-time into my role as an advisor dedicated to helping founders build better companies and teams.

Chris O'Byrne

How can somebody employ antifragile thinking in their current business?

Alex Snider

The optimal approach to consider is envisioning a pivotal point in the structure of process and systems—a sort of fulcrum that, when properly aligned, proves indispensable. However, it can become burdensome for an organization if not regularly reviewed. Engaging in processes without a clear understanding of the desired outcomes can result in operational complexities that surpass the needs of the business size. This realization became a decisive part of my learning journey. I discerned the key components that contributed to the success or failure of larger companies. Instead of attempting to impose a structure from one company onto another, regardless of their differences, I focused on comprehending the specific goals and available elements. This allowed me to construct a tailored and purposeful framework.

Applying the concept of antifragility involves understanding your company's strengths and the diverse ways they can be leveraged. It requires making decisions that align with your strengths while staying agile and responsive. Excessive adherence to processes on a singular focus can lead to oversight of valuable opportunities or over exposure and dependency to certain variables. Therefore, maintaining a balance and swiftly recognizing

and seizing opportunities is essential.

In terms of growth, expansion, and opportunities, understanding antifragility is akin to the concept that if you can't explain something, you don't truly know it. Your comprehension is lacking if you can't articulate it to a five-year-old. Understanding your capabilities and the breadth of applications allows you to pursue and build in line with your chosen strategy while remaining open to recognizing new opportunities or alchemizing a "loss" into an even bigger rebound opportunity.

A notable example of this adaptability is evident in the context of COVID. For instance, our focus was on immersive digital reality technology, often centered around virtual reality and large events. However, in-person events became obsolete when the pandemic hit, and the use of headsets declined sharply. Nevertheless, our expertise extended beyond virtual reality to augmented reality and a range of immersive tech. Leveraging our proficiency in organizing events and utilizing high-tech software, we identified alternative avenues.

Our approach involved recognizing that, although traditional virtual reality might not be feasible, we could employ augmented reality using the everyday smartphones that people were still very much attached to. Understanding our ability to use cutting-edge technology, we addressed practical and artistic needs. Typically, we applied gaming-level technology to solve business problems, but we also ventured into marketing and creative projects.

The key was identifying what individuals were aiming to achieve, whether practical or artistic, and determining how their goals can be supported through interactive experiences on a smartphone or using projection technology to keep things "hands free" and "touch free." While we had previously engaged in similar ventures with iPads, headsets, and other devices, this experience underscored the importance of adaptability and foresight.

So, we took that concept and decided that while people hesitated to touch physical objects, everyone still interacted with their phones. We saw an opportunity to create something valuable in that space. So that was one area we pivoted to. We also knew how to run engaging experience and events and had the tech to create virtual space. As a result, we were able to shift into creating events beyond the typical Zoom meetings.

We didn't just settle for basic online gatherings; instead, we looked at utilizing virtual space effectively. What engages people? How can we craft a holistic experience before and after the event? We repurposed techniques and tools we had previously used in different contexts, adapting them to our new virtual experiences. For instance, consider where physical product demonstrations were crucial, such as selling medical equipment to hospitals. With COVID restrictions preventing in-person visits, one couldn't simply send a representative to a hospital. Thus, we devised advanced virtual visit technology

with 3D renderings, animated models, video presentations, chat features, and online libraries. This allowed us to create a virtual showroom experience that successfully replaced traditional in-person visits.

Our approach wasn't about clinging to impractical solutions like outfitting everyone with VR headsets. Instead, we focused on identifying our core capabilities and principles, seeking ways to adapt and pivot effectively. This mindset influenced various aspects of our operations, from staffing strategies to innovative thinking.

Another example, from my previous corporate consulting role with a natural resources company, I discovered they were effectively operating an airline due to their remote locations which left them with an extremely rigid cost structure and inability to flex their operations to variations in staffing strategies or react to fluctuations in the commodities market.

Over time, they acquired a plane, built runways, and engaged in airline operations and aviation maintenance. It was suboptimal and super expensive. It became an unquestioned norm simply because it was the established status quo and seen as the way to achieve their goals but it made them at best 'robust' and frankly more 'fragile' as it stopped them

from being able to flex large parts of the operating cost.

When you embody antifragility, you break free from the cycle of, "This is how it's done because it has always been done that way," which seems functional until it's not. While it might be a bit of a stretch to attribute this directly to antifragility, the key lies in questioning the status quo, recognizing opportunities, and embracing experimentation.

In our case, we adopted a mindset of never letting a good disaster go to waste. When talented people faced job loss due to circumstances beyond their control, we seized the opportunity to bring them onto our team. We discovered emerging needs that weren't addressed by existing solutions, and we leveraged our skills to create new, tailored solutions. Similarly, questioning assumptions about how things should be done played a vital role in consulting. It wasn't about fulfilling the needs of X, Y, and Z; it was about approaching it in a way that truly mattered by understanding the underlying need and creating meaningful impact.

For example, questioning whether a company should focus on extracting resources from the ground or running an airline highlighted the distinction between two vastly different business models. Trying to

excel in both areas might not be efficient, yet decisions were made to own a plane without a clear alignment with the core business need—getting workers to site efficiently. Such a conventional approach may seem normal in diverse businesses, but it can be fundamentally ineffective and could potentially lead to operational collapse. Decisions made during times of prosperity, like when gold was valued at $1,800 an ounce, may become liabilities when economic conditions or operating context change, and adapting becomes difficult due to rigid, inflexible commitments to non-core activities.

Chris O'Byrne

Who were some of your key influences or mentors along the way?

Alex Snider

Mentors, in my view, come in various forms. During my consulting days, there were a few standouts, and David Walden was one such figure. As a partner in the company I joined, he held a prominent position in the sector I aspired to work in—mining, energy, and natural resources. Interestingly, I was initially assigned a mentor in the retail sector, which wasn't aligned with my career goals. Although the assigned mentor was great, I summoned the courage to approach David, a partner I had never met but admired, expressing my desire to work in his field.

I remember initiating the conversation, stating that I had already spent my first eight months in the industry, and I was keen on enhancing my involvement and expertise his domain. I straightforwardly asked if he would be willing to become my mentor. This encounter with David marked one of my initial and enduring lessons, which I continue to impart to my clients. He advised me of his working style and asked me to contact people he mentored, both within and outside the company. This practice, he emphasized, would provide valuable insights and perspectives.

I was receptive to this, and we had insightful discussions. So, I went and did that. Upon returning, I expressed my continued interest in being his mentee. He welcomed the idea, stating his willingness, but with a condition—I needed to take the initiative. He clarified that he wouldn't seek me out; instead, I should approach him, voice my needs, and set expectations.

Although the exact words might differ, this conversation, albeit a while back, marked the beginning of my journey in what I call "managing up." It's a practice that has significantly influenced my growth as a consultant, team member, and leader. I consistently require this mindset from those seeking to join my team or company. The benefits of opening bandwidth as a leader and gaining a broader perspective and responsibility as a team member are amazing.

David played an important role in my professional development, offering numerous opportunities and allowing me to contribute significantly by developing frameworks alongside him. Attending various pitches gave me crucial insight into how he interacted and managed a room. His mentorship extended beyond my time at that company; he is a skilled professional and someone I deeply respect and still look up to.

Another influential mentor was John Richard, a UK director I encountered during a project in Africa. Open conversations about anything and everything characterized our mentor-mentee relationship. Amidst the company's complexities, I could rely on him for genuine feedback, creating a relationship where I felt comfortable discussing and navigating challenges. John's exceptional storytelling ability and knack for uniting teams made our working styles harmonious, and our roles at that time brought us closer. Working with him was enjoyable and allowed me to be authentic. He saw me for who I was and appreciated my uniqueness, and that acceptance was crucial during that phase of my career.

The funny thing is I had an amazing client during my first role, Nicole Piggott, and we worked together intensely for about eight months on some challenging projects, fostering a close bond. Our professional relationship continued for about four years while she held executive positions. Notably, I also had the privilege of mentoring her remarkable daughter. We stayed connected for many years, and she eventually transitioned from corporate life to starting her own company, and more than a decade later she became a client again.

In reflection, I don't know if she realized she was a mentor to me because our dynamic was primarily as a client and consultant, characterized by a strong and collaborative relationship. Now, in my advisory role, she serves as CEO and business owner. Her influence on me was a unique blend of mentor and client roles. Observing her career journey and learning from her experiences proved fascinating despite their differences from mine. Traversing the corporate landscape alongside her, especially given the power dynamics inherent in

client-consultant relationships, gave me valuable insight.

Our interactions were genuine, with moments of difficulty where we consistently supported each other. Despite being extremely direct—a trait that can sometimes create tension among women today—we maintained a mutual understanding of our common interests and commitment to supporting each other through tough conversations. This experience significantly contributed to my professional development.

Reconnecting with her more actively over the past four months has been a wonderful experience. Amazingly, we've sustained this relationship for the better part of fifteen years, a testament to the enduring value of our connection.

Chris O'Byrne

What would you say was one of the most valuable lessons you learned from David?

Alex Snider

Identifying the most valuable lessons is a challenge given their multitude, but managing up stands out as particularly noteworthy. However, another key lesson revolves around the art of managing a room, emphasizing that success is as much about selecting moments for attentive listening and thoughtful silence as it is about choosing words and crafting compelling stories. This insight became evident through David's guidance, he was truly adept at storytelling, which he once attributed to his Irish ancestry. He demonstrated the power of narrative and imparted the wisdom of recognizing when to allow for silence and create space—acknowledging that effective leadership involves both leading and listening.

Chris O'Byrne

What parting words of wisdom would you give people?

Alex Snider

The crucial advice I often impart is the importance of cultivating self-awareness. Within this self-awareness, it's vital to balance audacity—an essential quality for entrepreneurs, driving the belief in creating something out of nothing—with humility. Entrepreneurial endeavors require a constant commitment and belief in success, yet it's equally important to shed any ego. Acknowledging that one can't be all-knowing or do everything alone is key.

Even when building A-teams, this self-awareness remains integral. It involves recognizing the limits of personal knowledge and skills and understanding when and where to seek support. Identifying areas where support is needed and being willing to ask for and accept it can be transformative. This shift in mindset has the potential to significantly impact personal and professional experiences, as well as the trajectory of one's business.

Action Steps

1. **Embrace and Cultivate Leadership Skills**: Inspired by the author's journey, focus on developing your leadership style. Recognize that effective leadership doesn't always require being the loudest voice in the room. Instead, it's about understanding and assigning roles, fostering team success, and ensuring everyone is informed and capable. This approach, a key part of servant leadership, prioritizes the success of the team as a whole, contributing to overall business growth and a positive work environment.

2. **Adapt and Strategize in Real-Time**: Reflecting on the author's athletic background, apply the same strategic thinking and adaptability to your business. This means constantly analyzing your business environment, measuring risks, and being willing to adapt strategies based on performance and market trends. Just like in sports, understanding your

team's strengths, studying your competitors, and exploiting opportunities as they arise can lead to significant business advancements.

3. **Leverage Personal Experiences for Business Innovation**: Utilize personal experiences and unique perspectives, just like the author did, to innovate in your business. The author's journey from athletics to entrepreneurship highlights the importance of resourcefulness and adaptability. This can involve reevaluating your business direction in uncertain times, exploring diverse opportunities, and applying lessons learned from personal challenges to create a resilient and innovative business model.

About the Author

Alex is a Strategic Growth & Leadership Coachsultant who assists seven and eight-figure founders in conquering their next level of business growth by gaining clarity on their vision and refining strategic decisions into actionable priorities in the realms of team growth, operational optimization, and sustainable business development. Her tailored approach empowers entrepreneurs to achieve profitable growth while stepping confidently into their zone of genius and fostering an engaged, self-sufficient team that delivers consistent results without micromanagement. Learn more at alexsnider.com.

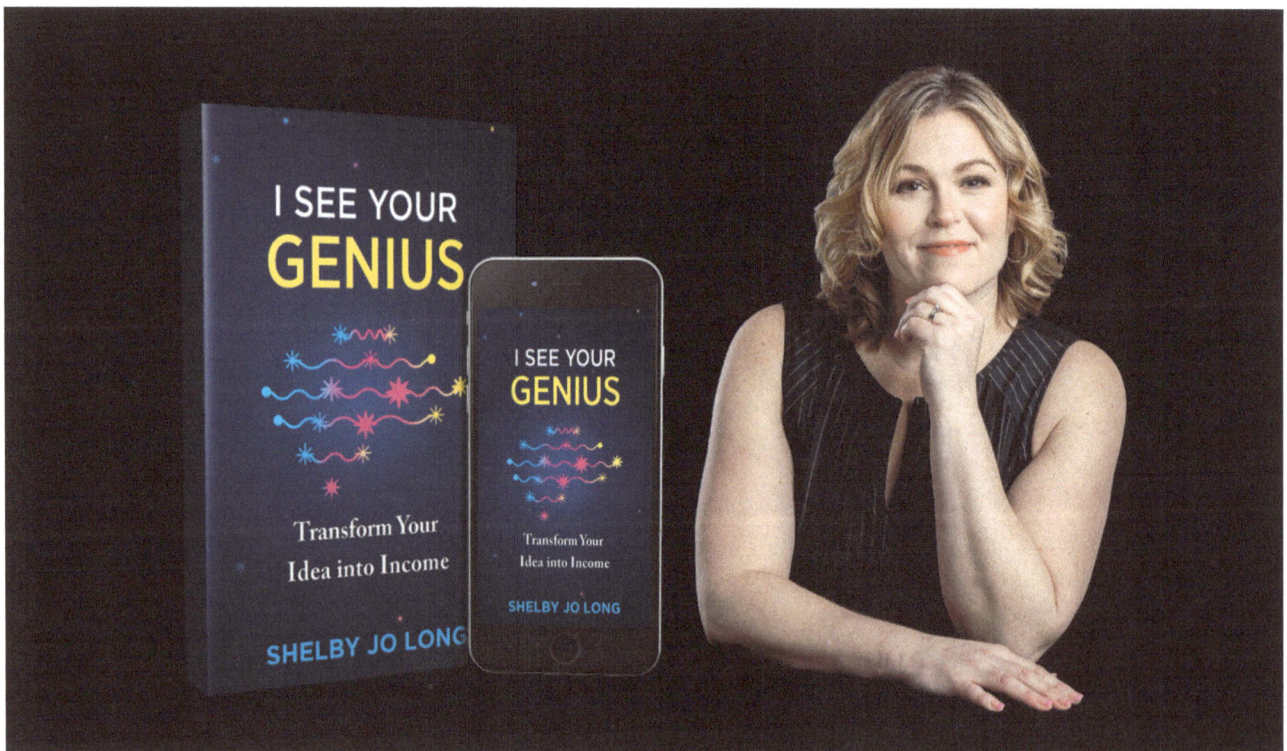

MICROCASTING

Supercharge Your Business!

Do you want to find new ways to add additional income to your coaching, consulting, or content creation business?

eLearning Portals by Microcasting is specifically designed for Coaches, Consultants, and Course Creators to engage your customers, establish yourself as a thought leader, and grow your revenues.

Here are just a few things you can do with **Microcasting**:

- ⊘ **Start selling** your courses and programs.
- ⊘ Create a **paid membership site** to grow your revenues.
- ⊘ Build a free membership site to **increase lead gen**.
- ⊘ Easily **integrate eLearning** into your marketing website.
- ⊘ Create **individualized customer portals** .
- ⊘ And so much more...

Microcasting is an all-in-one online learning platform that makes it easy for course creators to design, manage, and market their courses. With its personalized eLearning experience, you can keep your current customers engaged with your business, generating more upsells and higher renewal rates. Create courses quickly and effortlessly - all with the help of Microcasting!

Try Microcasting today and start transforming your business!

FROM CUSTOMER SERVICE TO SALES MASTERY

ROB DURANT

Chris O'Byrne

Can you share a story from childhood that helped shape who you are today?

Rob Durant

There's a book published by Dr. Seuss called *My Book About Me.* I owned a copy when I was seven. What made it special was that it was a hardcover book designed to be written in. It would ask, "How many steps are you from the nearest mailbox? How many steps are you from the nearest fire hydrant?" You'd fill in various pages with your answers. On one page, it asked, "What do you want to be when you grow up?" I still remember filling it out with one of those thick jumbo pencils, almost as wide as my thumb is now. I etched my responses into the pages as if I were carving them in stone - that's how seven-year-olds handle pencils.

First, I wrote *Cowboy.* Then, I erased it. Next, I wrote *Astronaut.* Again, I erased it. Finally, I settled on *Everything Man.* I aspired to be an everything man. Throughout my life, I've remained just as indecisive when it comes to what I want to be when I grow up. However, when I reflect on my career trajectory, it turns out that, in one way or another, I've indeed become an everything man.

I've had numerous opportunities spanning various roles and career paths, yet they all align with a common theme - at my core I am a helper. I am a teacher at heart, but was dissuaded from pursuing teaching as a professional career, given my father's experience as a math teacher in public schools for over fifty years. Witnessing his challenges while raising a family as a teacher, he wished for a different path for me. Though, had I expressed a strong desire to become a teacher, my father would have wholeheartedly supported me.

Instead, I moved on to other things. Despite my diverse roles, in each I consistently gravitated back to mentoring, leading, guiding, training - teaching. Embodying the essence of an everything man, in my career I've held many different roles. Yet, a discernible thread connects them all: I am, at my core, a helper.

Chris O'Byrne

Tell me about your transition from high school to where you are now.

Rob Durant

Attending college was always a given for me; being the son of a teacher, going to school was the pathway to a good job. However, I found myself uncertain about what I wanted to be or do - a common dilemma for many college and high school students. Amidst this uncertainty, however, one thing became clear. Because my family had the privilege of visiting Disney World several times during my middle and high school years I decided I wanted to work for Disney.

It was during one of these trips, just before graduating high school, that I struck up a conversation with one of the employees - I later learned they're called cast members. I asked how they landed their job at Disney World, my dream job. To me, this place embodied utopia. Everyone there seemed so, for lack of a better word, hopeful. The cast member shared details about the Disney College Program, an internship opportunity allowing college students to spend a semester at Disney World.

This was a game-changer for me. I chose my college because of its relationship with Disney World and its internship program. In my first eligible semester, which would have marked the beginning of my sophomore year, I applied, got accepted, and embarked on an internship instead of returning to campus. The experience resonated so deeply with me that, after completing my sophomore year at my initial school, I transferred schools to one just outside of Disney World. I concluded my college journey at the University of Central Florida in Orlando and went on to work at Disney World for nearly a decade - exactly what I had set out to do. The allure of being part of that vibrant community fueled my passion for the job.

After spending about a decade at Disney World, life took its course; I aged a bit, got married, and began raising a family. Being close to family became a priority for us. I have extended family in Boston and – to my surprise – they would not all uproot and relocate to Orlando.

Instead, my wife, our four-month-old newborn, and I moved back to Boston. Seeking employment, I briefly worked for Tiffany & Company, leveraging my extensive customer service experience from Disney. Enjoyable as it was, my stint at Tiffany was cut short because it was made clear to me that advancing into leadership required a move to their New Jersey corporate headquarters; this wasn't feasible given our recent relocation. I pursued other customer service roles. After a rigorous six-week interview process and batteries of tests, I secured a customer service position with the phone company.

To this day, I still remember the call I got from the HR representative offering me the role. I hesitated when she told me of the sales quota attached to the position. Despite my reservations, I accepted the job, admittedly unsure of what lay ahead. Until then, like many, I held a negative perception of sales, thinking "sales is evil", "sales is yucky." "Customer service wouldn't even be necessary if sales Sales didn't hadn't faltered".

As someone deeply rooted in customer service and inherently anti-sales, entering a sales role was intimidating. I was worried about losing the job, but then I remembered a valuable lesson— the art of outrunning the bear. When a bear is chasing you, you don't have to outrun the bear; you have to outrun those running beside you.

I was fortunate to be among the early hires, likely in the tenth cohort of new hires. At the time the phone company was hiring five to ten people each week. There were at least ten more cohorts following ours.

We received systems training and product training, but there was an absence of training in sales or customer service. Focusing on my strengths, I believed I could at least do a good job of retaining our existing customers by providing good customer service, helping me stay ahead of my peers in at least one aspect of the role.

In my view, delivering even adequate customer service

requires three essential elements: Ask questions, uncover the root cause of the issue, and present solutions so your customer can make an informed decision.

In sales, it turns out there are four things that outstanding salespeople do. Like with customer service, they ask questions, uncover the root cause of the issue, and present solutions so their prospects can make an informed decision.

There's one more thing that outstanding salespeople effortlessly perform, but customer service personnel struggle to execute: Asking for the sale. Most people in customer

service cannot bring themselves to do that.

I understand the reason behind their reluctance, as it used to be my struggle too. I would refrain from asking you, Chris, to buy something because I was personalizing the sale; I couldn't afford this, so I presumed you couldn't either, so in an effort to provide what I believed was outstanding customer service, I wouldn't insult you by asking you to buy it.

Then, one day, a simple yet powerful epiphany dawned on me. If we've identified the solution to their problem, it's *poor* customer service on my part not to let them access it. We don't lie, we don't cheat, and we don't steal - and a lie by omission is still a lie - but if together we have identified the root cause of the problem and a possible solution, even if the solution comes with an additional cost, customers are often willing to pay for it as it effectively addresses their problem. Or they may decide it's not worth the investment. Either way, as a customer service professional who provides options and asks, I've fulfilled my role, and we can proceed accordingly. And with that simple approach I became one of the most successful sellers in the company.

I have since taken on the role of educating other customer service professionals about sales. I thoroughly enjoy addressing customer service audiences. Typically, before the class commences, I engage with a "friendly" in the audience and say to them, "At the beginning of class I'm going to ask you for your wallet, and you're going to give it to me, even though it may sound absurd."

As the class begins, I incorporate a quick story into my introduction. I ask my accomplice for their wallet (let's call him Matt), and to everyone's surprise, he hands it over. I then announce, "We're going to lunch at this burger place, but we're not going to invite Matt because he can't afford it." Appalled and angered, I tell my audience they've given me the exact reactions I was hoping for. I then go on to a draw parallel between that and my story of not selling in the name of "outstanding" customer service.

As I mentioned, I did considerably well as a salesperson, earning bonuses, prizes, presidents' club trips, and more. However, true to my nature, I found myself drawn to helping others and moved into leadership and training roles. From customer service at Disney to roles in sales and sales leadership with the phone company and beyond, to me, I still view each as a form of customer service.

I'm pleased to note that the sales industry is evolving too, moving away from the traditional "type A" mentality of being able to sell anything to anyone – whether they need it or not. Instead, there's a growing emphasis on a servant-sales role. Today, success is achieved by a commitment to serving others rather than simply closing deals at all costs.

My current company, Flywheel Results, emerged during the pandemic. After a decade with the phone company, I transitioned into teaching, spending time in public education, teaching math and business. Despite the challenges of raising a family as a teacher, I found fulfillment in the role.

Unexpectedly, a recruiter contacted me through LinkedIn during the summer of my second year in public schools. She was working with a VP at a tech startup seeking a math teacher, as their sales team "didn't know math". I laughed, but I couldn't resist the allure of working with a tech startup and fulfilling one of my (at the time) three career bucket list goals. It's not often your bucket list calls and says, "We want you."

I took the interview, landed the job, and discovered my passion for the startup world. The beauty of startups lies in the endless possibilities. There's no resistance to new ideas, because they're still charting their course. They don't have decades of institutional practices holding back innovation.

I was tasked with accelerating sales. We were building the roads while still determining the road map. Successfully navigating this hypergrowth phase, we achieved remarkable results. The pattern repeated in my second startup, delivering even faster results. I was able to recognize even greater results with my third startup and had a great long-term trajectory with the organization until the pandemic derailed that plan.

That's when I realized I instead of repeating this process within a different organization every twelve to eighteen months, why not make it a lifelong commitment with just one job? That's why Flywheel Results was launched. Whether aiding startups through hypergrowth, developing sales playbooks, building sales enablement frameworks, or conducting sales training sessions - including my current favorite, teaching social enablement, I get to be the everything man that seven-year-old me dreamed of becoming.

Chris O'Byrne

What was the third item on your bucket list?

Rob Durant

I'm glad you circled back to that. My three bucket-list career goals were: teaching (which I was already doing), working for a startup (which came knocking at my door), and working for a major consulting group. However, I learned that those roles generally require extensive travel - flying out on a Sunday night and returning on Friday night, leaving just about a day and a half with my family. This lifestyle wasn't conducive to what I desired. Interestingly, I ended up checking that off my bucket list by establishing my startup – without the travel. Essentially, I am a consultant, but it's for my venture rather someone else's company.

Chris O'Byrne

What is social enablement, and how does somebody leverage it?

Rob Durant

If I labeled it "social selling," a term widely used in the industry today, it might evoke the vibe of that Carly Rae Jepsen song: "Hey, we just connected, and this is crazy, but here's my sales pitch, so buy some maybe." And let's face it, nobody will buy into that. So, I prefer not to term it a social selling methodology.

It's social enablement because it's not about that hard sell; it's about being approachable, being sociable, and being generous. When you embody these qualities, people find you likable. As it turns out, people prefer doing business with people they like. Our clients secure deals that are 30% larger and 40% faster - all without resorting to the typical connect-and-pitch. My upcoming book centers around this concept: *Stop Pitching, Start Selling: The Social Enablement Blueprint.*

It explains what I mean by being approachable. What does it mean to be sociable? What does it mean to be generous? And how do I leverage these qualities toward commercial results? While it is about achieving commercial success, it's not about delivering a pitch slap. It's about my understanding of you, what you offer, and your target business connections. It's also about leaving you with an understanding of what I offer and how I can contribute to your business goals.

As an adjunct at Northeastern University delivering an Introduction to Marketing class, I'm still actively involved in teaching. I particularly enjoy sharing with my students insights about success in life.

Success in life isn't solely about what you know. Northeastern is a highly selective school. The journey for these students thus far has pretty much revolved solely around what they know - classes taken, tests they've passed, SAT and AP scores. Then here I come to tell them that success is not solely dictated by knowledge.

Some might say, "So it's about networking and nepotism." Fortunately, success in life isn't just about who you know either. You could know everyone, but if you know nothing, are you someone worth knowing?

Success is about who knows you for what you know. Your job, then, is to ensure that more and more people recognize you for what you know. Social enablement is the process that facilitates this.

In your Rolodex you probably have a good doctor, a sharp lawyer, and, if you're lucky, a trustworthy mechanic. Who is in your Rolodex for what I want to be known for? I want to make sure that's me. Who is in my Rolodex for what you want to be known for? You want to make sure that's you. That's where being sociable comes in.

When we talk, I will get to know you. But I won't pitch you anything. You probably have no immediate need for social enablement solutions anyway. However, three conversations later, you might find yourself discussing the aversion to the pitch-slap with someone. You'll recall, "I was just talking with somebody about how much we hate the pitch-slap, and he's got a solution for it." You'll facilitate an introduction because you remember me and the good conversation we had. That's what it means to leverage social enablement - to be approachable, to be sociable, and to be generous. Commercial opportunities will naturally present themselves.

Here's the thing. We all know about karma and good karma. What I'm doing is not groundbreaking. Dale Carnegie wrote the book *How to Win Friends and Influence People* eighty-seven years ago. Today, some view that title as somewhat

manipulative, but it wasn't meant that way when written.

There's nothing about manipulation in social enablement either. It's simply a way of putting formal methods in place for those who say, "I would love to do get more business from the social platforms, but I don't know how to start." Here's the blueprint on how to do that.

Chris O'Byrne

What does Flywheel Results provide?

Rob Durant

We provide consulting, training, and coaching for sales organizations. What I like to say is if you are a VC, a founder, or a sales leader aiming to enhance your sales results not just incrementally but exponentially, I would love to have a conversation with you.

Chris O'Byrne

Along the way, I'm sure you've had many people who have influenced you. Who were some of those people who helped guide you?

Rob Durant

My father served as my most influential mentor and guide. I've been fortunate to learn about customer service from exceptional individuals and leaders. In sales, my experiences have included positive and negative examples. However, those customer service-first leaders truly shaped my approach to sales.

The VP of Sales who was looking for someone with a math background, and his willingness to take a chance on me despite no previous startup experience proved pivotal for me. I'm sincerely grateful for that opportunity. Our collaboration led to significant achievements.

Before I joined, they had been languishing for about a year in what should have been their exponential growth phase. At the time they had a staggering 60% turnover in their salesforce. A 60% turnover meant when they hired someone in January they were rehiring for the same seat in June. As I like to say, "Empty seats don't fill a quota."

Implementing processes and frameworks, we successfully reduced turnover to less than 10%, closer to 5%. We expanded the sales team from 10 to 50, increased the number of people meeting the quota, and while nearly doubling the quota itself.

Can I claim sole credit for this success? No. While I'd love to take a victory lap, it was about having the right people in the right places, willing to collaborate, listen, and contribute to the process. Amid various positive and negative influences, this VP stands out as someone who gave me the chance for which I'm eternally grateful.

Chris O'Byrne

What did you do at Disney?

Rob Durant

I began my career working in the American Adventure at Epcot Center's World Showcase. Over time, I had the opportunity to work at all the attractions in the World Showcase area, collaborating with international students, which I found immensely rewarding. After that, I transitioned to their central reservation office, gaining valuable call center experience. Returning to the parks, I worked in guest relations on Main Street USA. In my final role there, I handled correspondence in the Guest Communications office. This was in the era when email was just emerging, and most people sent letters. If you mailed a letter to Disney World, you received a written response, and my role involved composing those responses.

Chris O'Byrne

What are the most valuable lessons that you've learned along the way?

Rob Durant

I've discovered that even if you consider yourself an introvert, overcoming it and finding your voice is crucial. Knowing everything is of little use if others aren't aware of what you know. Sharing your voice isn't as challenging as it may seem, and remember, they can't eat you.

Expressing opinions that others may disagree with is okay, and fearing what others think should not hinder you from speaking up. Even though I am a self-professed

Chris O'Byrne

How does somebody go about finding their voice?

Rob Durant

I wish I could tell you, but I don't know. I can share what motivated me. Upon being hired for my internship at Walt Disney World, I was placed at the American Adventure, my dream job. On day two, they handed me a spiel

speaking. Interestingly, it took only one year after high school graduation to find myself doing this at Disney, with one year of college in between. Around that same time, my sister, two years younger, wrote a college essay expressing her admiration for my ability to speak in front of audiences. She remembered me as the guy too shy to order Domino's Pizza over the phone.

introvert (or ambivert, as some may say), I am outgoing when necessary. However, I want my downtime and quiet moments because, at times, mustering the energy to be social can be difficult. Nevertheless, it's too important not to engage.

to deliver to the audience. I was tasked with memorizing a page of text and present it to a crowd of around 1,000 people every hour.

I found my voice because my desire to be part of Disney exceeded my fear of public

How can others find their voice? Put yourself out there. Give it a try. Explore different avenues. I'm here to help; reach out, and we can put your voice out in various shapes and forms together. The key is to find a way, and through that, you'll discover your audience.

Chris O'Byrne

It's like people who do podcasts. Many mention the initial awkwardness of figuring things out, but there's usually a point where they find their groove—where they discover their voice. I've heard this sentiment countless times from people sharing their podcasting journey. What words of wisdom can you offer on this?

Rob Durant

I don't know that I have any because I don't want to deter you from discovering your wisdom. You already know what is essential to you, what you want to be doing, and how to go about it. Perhaps you've forgotten; we tend to be focused on our tasks and that can cause a lack of self-awareness.

I encourage people to take the time; the new year is an opportune moment for this reflection. I often encourage people to reassess their "why." I regularly incorporate Simon Sinek's video "Start with Why" into my classes, presenting it within the first thirty minutes of each new course, be it in a formal classroom or a corporate setting. Subsequently, I prompt participants to reflect on why they are present.

I encourage everyone to regularly scrutinize their motivations: Why am I doing this? I then share with them the concept of the "five whys." After you answer question "Why am I doing this?", continue asking why for each following response. By about the fifth why, you often encounter answers such as "Because that's the way we've always done it." This revelation serves as a starting point for further exploitation, leading to questions like, "Why have we always done it this way?" and "What else can we do?"

These insights are not my words of wisdom but yours. The wisdom emerges when you take the time to sit down and listen to yourself.

Action Steps

1. **Explore Diverse Career Opportunities:** Reflect on the author's journey and consider diversifying your own career path. Embrace different roles and opportunities, even if they seem unrelated to your current business. This broadens your skill set and perspective, potentially leading to innovative approaches and solutions within your business.

2. **Enhance Customer Service with Sales Skills:** Drawing inspiration from the author's transition from customer service to sales, improve your business by integrating sales techniques into your customer service strategy. Train your team to not only address customer needs but also to identify opportunities for additional sales, without compromising on service quality.

3. **Invest in Personal Development and Networking:** The author's story emphasizes the importance of finding one's voice and building a network. Work on personal development, particularly in areas like public speaking and social skills. Simultaneously, focus on expanding your professional network. This not only improves your own capabilities but also increases the visibility and influence of your business.

About the Author

At his core, Rob Durant is a teacher. He guides sales organizations through sales hyper-growth and help build unicorns. Learn more at flywheelresults.com.

RSS RELIABLE
STAFF SOLUTIONS

www.ReliableStaffSolutions.com

RISING THROUGH RESILIENCE AND OVERCOMING ADVERSITY

MELANIE HERSCHORN

Chris O'Byrne:

What was something from your childhood that helped you become who you are today?

Melanie Herschorn:

I always felt invisible. I felt like I had all these giant aspirations to be a star, but I felt like I had to be a good girl. The messages I received were: Do your homework, get straight A's, do what we tell you, and become a doctor someday. However, that didn't fit who I was or who I am. I didn't realize the profound impact that would have on me as an adult. I had to work through a lot of head trash because I thought I would never be what I wanted to be if I was not the professional my family expected me to be. Thankfully, I've worked through it. I make jokes about it now, so I know I'm okay.

Chris O'Byrne:

How did you work through the head trash?

Melanie Herschorn:

I had a "come to Jesus" moment, which wasn't that long ago. About a year ago, I had a conversation with one of my parents, which set me off. I was crying. I didn't understand the gravity of what I'd been living with. I finally realized that I had internalized my parents' beliefs about what success looks like. When I could say, "Hold on, that's not how I feel," I could let it go.

Chris O'Byrne:

What was your journey from graduating high school to where you are now?

Melanie Herschorn:

It was not linear. I went to the University of Toronto because I was living in Canada, so attending a Canadian school made sense. My parents told me, "If you want to be a journalist, you need to learn everything about the world ahead of time, so you need to study history." I agreed. I remember sitting on the subway and reading through the course syllabus. This was in the 90s, so things were printed because the internet was still new. It was this thick book made of newsprint. I read through it, looked at all the history classes, and thought about how interesting it was and how I would love to learn more. I got excited about history and decided to pursue it.

I do not regret that because I thought I knew everything when I graduated high school. When I started college, I realized I knew nothing. College was very eye-opening and wonderful. Now, I can tell you many fascinating facts you might or might not know about things that happened in early modern Europe. But more importantly, it opened the world to me in a way that studying communications would not have.

When I graduated from college, I was dating a guy long-distance. He was living in Los Angeles, and I was in Toronto. I planned to leave Canada for good and move to LA. I didn't know what to do when I got out there, and a friend suggested I look into public relations. She thought I'd be good at it. The universe gives you these guides, and you don't even realize it's happening. I still do public relations to this day. And if not for my friend Tracy, I don't know if I ever would have found it.

I managed to get myself an internship at a boutique celebrity PR firm, and I then parlayed that into a job. I was walking red carpets with celebrities. I was even on a reality show on Bravo one year. There was the exciting part, the red carpet. Then there was the not-exciting part, dealing with unhappy celebrities. On my twenty-fourth birthday, I was told off twice by a comedian for something I hadn't actually done. And I thought, *I think I'm done with this. I want to do something where people respect me and the work I'm putting in.*

I got a call from my mother not long after that happened. I was still living in LA at the time, and she was in Toronto. She told me she found some Post-its I had written notes on about graduate schools for journalism. She wanted to give them to me because she thought they were from my most recent trip home. But they were seven years old! I had been toying with the idea of going back to school to get a master's in journalism, and she called me holding Post-it notes that I had written seven years prior about possibly getting my master's in journalism. Again, hi, Universe.

I started applying to schools and got into the University of Southern California. That changed my career trajectory because I graduated at the top of my class.

After graduation, I moved to Pennsylvania, where my husband was living. We were apart for the first year of marriage. I got the first job I applied to out of graduate school at the local NPR affiliate in Harrisburg, Pennsylvania, and they had an opening for a classical music announcer. I had no idea how to do that, but I figured it was an in. I had been on the radio in undergrad, but that was my only experience in radio. But they hired me and then moved me after about eight months to news when there was an opening. I was the afternoon news anchor and reporter. It was amazing and stressful. I did it for a couple of years, but I was newly married and wanted to have a baby. I was ready. I was thirty-one at the time, so we planned, as much as you can plan, to have a baby in a non-election year. As the only woman in the newsroom, there was pressure not to take time off, even for becoming a mom. When I was five months pregnant, I got laid off. They say (wo)man plans and God laughs. Luckily, the local newspaper scooped me up and brought me on as a freelancer on the school district beat. It was a great gig for that time in my life.

My husband got a job in Phoenix, and we moved. When I got here, I thought about trying to get a job as a reporter, but we'd have to pay a nanny or daycare more money than I'd ever make as a journalist. I also thought about trying something else because had this idea I couldn't shake. It was to design and manufacture breastfeeding clothing.

My whole purpose on this planet is to take people who are feeling bad about themselves in whatever way—whether it's an underdog who doesn't get their

story reported or a new mom who feels bad about herself and just wants to feel good again, even though her body is still not her own. Now, I help business owners who become authors and want to get their message out in the world but don't know how. This is the through line of my life. I love to support people. It makes

my heart shine. When I started designing breastfeeding clothing, I didn't know what I was doing, so I Googled my way through it. I was at the biggest trade shows, standing on the floor by myself. I sold my clothes on Nordstrom. com.. I sold on Amazon and in boutiques in Canada and the US. I was doing it. I was not necessarily

doing it correctly. I should have asked for help, but I didn't. When I finally did ask for help, I learned a valuable lesson because that help drove my business into the ground, and I had to close it.

Chris O'Byrne:

What happened to make you close your business?

Melanie Herschorn:

I met a woman who was doing celebrity gifting suites to get celebrity endorsements. As a vendor, you give away all your stuff in exchange for social media posts or photos with celebrities. The celebrity goes from table to table to table, and they ask what you do. Then you tell them, "I have this really great thing I'd love for you to try. Hey, can I get a picture with you?" They're like, "Sure, thanks for your free thing."

A few years later, the gifting suite woman said, "I'm marketing for baby brands, and you need my help." I said, "All right, tell me more." She sold me a whole bill of goods, and I said, "You're right. I do need that." Unfortunately, I did not need that. Over a year, I paid her about $25,000. I had 7,000 Instagram followers who were not buying my clothes. The worst part of all was how manipulative and emotionally abusive she was to me.

In the end, I couldn't open the office door, and the office was in my house. It wasn't a big house. I decided to close the business for several reasons. At the time, millennial moms had stopped wearing what I was producing, and they were more interested in getting fast fashion that they could throw out later. I could see that piece of it, but I was emotionally wrecked. I started to believe what she would say, like, "Melanie, how do you have a master's degree? You're so boring. Your writing is so terrible." My husband said, "But you're paying her!" I said, "I know, but I'm afraid. What if she tries to ruin me and do a smear campaign online?" Of course, now I know better. But then I didn't. I was deeply entrenched.

I watched a documentary about this film producer named Randall Emmett, and he's the ex of a reality star. He ran a shady operation in Hollywood, and he would get his assistants to do insane things. In one instance, he had his assistant get a bunch of drugs out of a safe in a hotel room, and the assistant could have been arrested. The assistant was basically brainwashed to believe that this was okay, and this is how it's done. They fear they'll lose everything if they don't measure up. It's that feeling. I felt that, too. Having worked in that entertainment business, I know what that's like. You think your life is ruined if you don't do the stupidest, most minute thing for your boss. That's the mentality of it. I easily slipped

back in when this Hollywood woman behaved the way she did.

Chris O'Byrne:

This is very valuable to anybody reading this because I bet many people are going through the same thing.

Melanie Herschorn:

Especially with marketing, because so many people will sell you things you want to hear, and they don't deliver and never will. But they'll take your money. When I closed the business, I thought, *What can I do now?* I didn't feel like a phoenix rising from the ashes.

However, I had an idea. I could help people with their marketing in a supportive way. I decided to metaphorically hang a shingle and say, "I'm going to be a marketer now." When authors started calling, I realized there was something to it. I've been helping authors ever since. I'm an author now, which was a lifelong dream. It's been a magical ride.

Chris O'Byrne:

How do you help authors today?

Melanie Herschorn:

They don't have to be authors yet; they can just be thinking they want to be an author. There has to either be a book in your mind or a book in existence. The truth is, book sales won't make you rich. Most people only make a few dollars from each book sold, so it doesn't add up quickly. We examine the whole strategy and how authors can leverage their books to create new revenue streams. These could include courses or programs, higher speaking fees, getting on stages they couldn't get on without a book, or media opportunities that help get even more eyes on their book, mission, and business.

I help authors who have already written books and haven't seen much traction to develop a robust marketing strategy that gets them the results they had hoped for. I've also partnered with a publisher to help take authors through the entire process. From the idea in their mind to writing it, editing it, publishing it, and marketing it in one fell swoop. The goal is to see the book as an opportunity, not an end.

I'm not going to take your money if I can't help you, but I'm also going to tell you, "Don't give your money to so and so because they're not going to help you either. Here are the things that will help you best." I'm such a fan of self-publishing and hybrid publishing because you, as the author, have the control. I had a client who really want to publish with a traditional publisher. She submitted her thirty-five-page proposal. She got a very small advance, and then they made her wait fourteen months before

publishing the book. Imagine if this book was about AI. It wasn't, but imagine if it was. It would have been obsolete before it was ever published.

Chris O'Byrne:

Let's say an author comes to you and has an idea for a book and knows they want to use their book to generate leads and get more business; they understand that much. What does that process look like for you working with them?

Melanie Herschorn:

First, we take you through the book-writing process. We have all these tips and tricks to get the book out of you and on paper. Then, we set you up with editors who will edit your book because your book needs and deserves a good editor.

Then, we will get you set up with a book formatter. I didn't fully grasp how vital that part was until I published my book and that's why you need an expert to guide you as a new author. You don't know what you don't know.

Also, we help get your cover professionally designed. We judge books by their covers. So, all that is set up. Then, you self-publish under your imprint, and we help you through that. While all that is happening, you are building your marketing foundation so that the minute

the book is ready, you are getting media opportunities, speaking opportunities, podcast guesting opportunities, and real, genuine reviews on Amazon because those count. It's a group/one-on-one hybrid, and people can join anytime.

Chris O'Byrne:

What will be expected of them? What work will they need to put in?

Melanie Herschorn:

You will get strategy and support. You will write your book unless you want someone to write it for you, in which case, we know many great ghostwriters who can write the book for you. However, if you are ready to do the writing yourself, that's what we'll help you do. The editing is not on your plate. We do that. We will get you the cover and the formatting done. It will be done for you. You don't have to do that yourself. We help you self publish, which means publishing your book under your own imprint. We show you how to do the marketing, and you can have your VA implement it or implement it yourself. We will have social media graphics available for you and create a press release for you. We write the press release and put it out in the media. There are several bonuses and a best-seller campaign, which people like. Of course, being a bestseller is not a marketing plan in and of itself. All these pieces are part of our program the Red Carpet Author Experience.

Then there are the people who have already written a book. They wrote it six months ago. They wrote it three years ago. It's making them feel bad about themselves because nothing's happened. They know they spent so much time and money and just feel like, *What can I do to get my book out in the world?* We have a marketing program called The Impactful Author just for you to take the book and start gaining that traction. That also is a group, one-on-one hybrid because everybody needs one-on-one attention, but I strongly believe in the importance of community as an author. We can help each other because we'll often face the same challenges, and the camaraderie makes this less of a lonely endeavor.

Chris O'Byrne:

What is some parting advice you can leave people with?

Melanie Herschorn:

The journey to becoming an author can be overwhelming. That's why I'm here to support new authors every step of the way. One thing I've noticed is that the marketing piece gets missed a lot. People often say, "I should market my book, but I don't know how, so I'm just not going to." I can break it down so you understand how to do it. Marketing means telling people about it. It's how people learn about your book because if they don't know you wrote a book, they won't buy it. If you're using social media for your marketing already, start talking about your book. If you're using email marketing already, start talking about your book. Remember to leverage other people's audiences as part of your marketing. Go on podcasts. You can be part of many free summits, and the only entrance fee is sending out emails to your list. It costs nothing except your time, but you can let more people know about your book.

The final thing I'll say is your book doesn't fall off a cliff once it's published. No matter when you wrote it, if the content is still relevant, keep sharing it.

Action Steps

1. **Change How You View Success**: Think about the author's story and how she changed her idea of success. Ask yourself if your business goals really match what you enjoy and care about. Sometimes success isn't just about making money, but also about doing what makes you happy and fulfilled.

2. **Try New Paths**: The author didn't follow a straight path; she tried different things before finding what worked for her. In your business, this means being open to new ideas. Maybe you can try new ways to market your products or services, or maybe you can offer something different that no one else is doing.

3. **Learn from Tough Times**: The article shows how the author got through hard times and came out stronger. In your business, when things don't go as planned, instead of giving up, look for what you can learn from these experiences. This could be about making your marketing better, improving how you talk to customers, or changing parts of your business that aren't working well. Every problem can teach you something and help you grow.

About the Author

Melanie Herschorn wants to help you step into your spotlight as an author. As a book marketing and publishing strategist for business owners, coaches, consultants, and speakers worldwide, she's on a mission to empower authors to share their message with the world. Get your ultimate book marketing checklist at vipbookmarketing.com/checklist.

EMPOWERING WOMEN IN BUSINESS TO UNLEASH THEIR AUTHENTIC GENIUS

★★★★★

Program is 🔥

Results and ROI! These ladies and their team are the real deal.
★★★★★

AUTHENTIC GENIUS PROGRAM

WHAT'S INCLUDED

- Monthly Business Coaching
- Authentic Genius Book
- Authentic Genius Magazine Feature
- TEDx Training & Signature Keynote
- Book Signing
- Branding and Marketing
- PR Positioning

✉ JULIEMDUCHARME@GMAIL.COM

✉ SHELBY@BUSINESSDYNAMICS.AGENCY

ABOUT THE PROGRAM

Your Authentic Genius is a groundbreaking *12-month program* led by Dr. Julie Ducharme and Shelby Jo Long. This unique program is designed exclusively for female business leaders, aiming to propel them to the next level in their professional and personal journeys. The program offers a comprehensive approach that covers business and leadership coaching, branding, scaling, book authorship, keynote speaking, and public engagement.

MASTERING THE DIGITAL WORLD WITH SEO AND PAID SEARCH

MICHAEL FLEISCHNER

Chris O'Byrne

What's the big picture of what you do from a business perspective, and why is that important for people to know?

Michael

From a business perspective, we operate as a digital marketing agency specializing in SEO and paid search management. The significance of our work lies in our mission to help individuals and companies present their best online image.

Over nearly two decades of experience, I've discovered that the most effective approach, aside from social media—which is somewhat distinct—is a synergistic blend of SEO and paid search. This could involve social media paid search or platforms like Google Ads. Individuals and businesses can significantly enhance their visibility by strategically utilizing paid and organic search, including Google Business and organic Google rankings.

I often emphasize that you are defined by what Google says about you, a statement that holds true. Being mindful about your online presence is crucial in today's business landscape. In reality, no one is exempt from this consideration. This aspect is particularly evident given the diverse range of companies we handle at our agency.

Occasionally, someone within a business might argue, "It doesn't matter what people say about me online. Nobody can find me anyway; I have a common name." That's understandable, but in just a minute and a half, I can locate your online listings. Wouldn't it be preferable to be proactive and control that narrative?

I believe that's the essence of our work: safeguarding the online reputations of individuals and companies and recognizing the paramount importance it holds in today's digital landscape.

Chris O'Byrne

How would you summarize that? Would you say that you help find people—and get found in the right way—online?

Michael

I believe that's a fantastic way to articulate it. We amplify someone's online visibility, ensuring that the presented information casts them in the best possible light. It's crucial to exercise caution in this regard, as the power of online presence can be used for both positive and negative purposes. We're very selective about who we work with, emphasizing our business's dual challenge and benefit. We strive to distinguish the deserving entities, those morally and ethically aligned with positive actions, and actively support them in becoming prominently visible online.

Chris O'Byrne

Why is that important to you?

Michael

I think it boils down to our core values. We strive to do the right thing and treat others as we would like to be treated. Culturally, we are inclined to support businesses, individuals, and corporations engaged in positive endeavors within our agency. Fortunately, such entities are abundant, ensuring that we'll always have meaningful work. This allows us the privilege of being discerning, choosing to align with clients who share our vision for making a positive impact in the world rather than attempting to cater to everyone.

Chris O'Byrne

Do you have a story from childhood that shaped who you are today?

Michael

There are a few pivotal moments in my life that, upon reflection, I believe significantly shaped my path. One such moment was the loss of my mom at what I considered a very young age. I was nineteen at the time, and her passing was unexpected and tragic. It took me many years to navigate through the grief and attempt to comprehend its implications for my life.

I've come to recognize the significance of a specific type of nurturing relationship—essential not only on a personal level but also in the business realm. Combining this insight with my nearly two decades of experience in the corporate world, working with sizeable companies and fostering numerous relationships with diverse agencies, I pondered what I wanted to do differently.

I won't claim superiority, as numerous robust agencies exist, particularly in the digital marketing domain. Instead of striving for improvement, the focus should be on conducting operations consistent with your core values, where you believe you can deliver the highest value to a specific client or customer in the market.

I feel like this philosophy underlies the essence of Big Fin SEO. If I may digress for just a minute to discuss search engine optimization, we've experienced both highs and lows as an industry. SEO has long been a critical component of everyone's marketing strategy, a significance that persists today. However, it got a bad rap in its early days due to its susceptibility to manipulation.

As a result, numerous companies, including many from overseas and some with questionable practices, flooded the SEO industry. This influx casts a shadow over the entire concept of SEO, even though its importance remains as significant, if not more so, than ever. The landscape has evolved, making manipulation less straightforward than it once was.

Some people have hesitated to engage with it, citing its complexity as a reason to avoid it. We thrive on the challenge because of its enduring impact on companies and individuals who prioritize it in their strategies.

I believe now is the best time to be in SEO, although some may dispute this. The truth is Google is currently incentivizing companies that create high-quality assets, be it information, videos, images, blog posts, and more. I see the industry aligning in the right direction, recognizing and rewarding companies that consistently produce the most engaging and value-added content.

Chris O'Byrne

What's the path that led you to establishing Big Fin SEO?

Michael

Big Fin was essentially my freelance business for a considerable period while working in corporate America. My story may not be unique; I ascended through the ranks, eventually managing large marketing departments for major publishers and education technology companies.

However, I felt the need for something more, a desire for fulfillment in focusing on my passion, which, at the time, was writing and editing. I began freelancing on the side, taking on small jobs here and there. As one thing led to another, one client referred me to another, and it kept growing from there.

I found it challenging to balance both worlds—working full-time from 8:00 a.m. to 6:00 p.m. and then freelancing for extended hours to pursue my passion. Given my risk-averse nature at the time, I made a decision. I told myself that if I could earn the same amount of money freelancing as I did in my full-time job, I would leave the latter. It served as a safety net for me. In my mind, the idea of earning anywhere close to my full-time job seemed improbable, providing me with a sense of reassurance.

Fast-forward a couple of years, maybe two or three years into it, and I was earning the same amount freelancing as my full-time job. Some friends, who were aware of my story, suggested, "Why not continue doing both? It's like doubling your salary." The answer is that it was unsustainable. Juggling two full-time jobs was overwhelming.

After many sleepless nights, I quit my full-time job and transitioned into a full-time freelancing career. I leaped, and over three years, I experienced substantial growth. The first year was a bit slow, but by the second year, I performed

well. In the third year, I was fully established and thriving.

Upon introspection, I realized that being a full-time freelancer wasn't meeting my expectations. I reached a point where I was not only providing assistance and delivering value but also handling sales, marketing, accounting, customer service, and fulfillment—essentially running an entire business independently. At that juncture, I contemplated whether it might be easier to return to corporate America.

That's pretty much what transpired. I re-entered corporate life, securing a senior leadership position at an HR company. I dedicated four years to this role until an unexpected challenge surfaced; the company underwent acquisition, leading to the termination of all executives, including me. Experiencing job loss for the first time, I resolved to persist in the corporate realm and immediately began searching for a new job.

However, I first discovered that the job market proved more challenging than I had anticipated, particularly given my specialization within the industry. The salary I had grown accustomed to became a hindrance, making it difficult to secure a position. Faced with this predicament, I resorted to freelancing again, driven by desperation and the need to adapt to the circumstances.

I embarked on this journey once again but with a different approach. I entered the endeavor with a clear perspective, determined to prioritize delivering value. I envisioned a trajectory where, as the business expanded, I would progressively bring in individuals to form a team composed of freelancers. This vision materialized in establishing the full-fledged agency Big Fin SEO, which is where we find ourselves today. I often reflect that if it weren't for being unexpectedly removed from the corporate ladder, I might not be in this position today, and Big Fin, in its current form, might not exist. I appreciate those unforeseen events because sometimes, a gentle push is all you need to navigate a particular path. I believe that push was what I required.

Chris O'Byrne

Many agency owners encounter difficulties launching their businesses, often functioning more like glorified freelancers. While they may label it a business, it remains a one-person show. How did you navigate the path to building a truly successful agency?

Michael

The pivotal factor for me was pinpointing my skill set and determining the quickest, most effective route to growth. Having spent numerous years in corporate America, I have cultivated many agency relationships. Despite not being inherently a salesperson—a skill I've since developed—I was initially uncomfortable and not proficient at it. I didn't see the value in pressuring someone to buy my offer. While my approach has evolved, my fundamental decision remains consistent: I prefer engaging in meaningful work.

At Big Fin, we thrive on collaborating as a partner with other marketing agencies. Many agencies lack full-time SEOs or dedicated paid search managers due to the associated costs, especially with the high expenses of proficient individuals. Recognizing this gap, we have carved our path to growth by strategically leveraging relationships with other agencies, essentially serving as their white-label solution.

I must note that while our current position results from these strategies, moving forward, we are diversifying our approach to acquiring new clients. This includes initiatives such as cold emailing and running targeted ads for specific offers. As our business has expanded, so has our marketing and outreach. But it's essential to acknowledge that our initial success stemmed from these strategic agency relationships, which were genuinely a win-win scenario.

They could offer SEO to their clients, and in turn, we provided the agencies with a service that seamlessly complemented their offerings. As an agency, we enjoyed a consistent flow of business that didn't necessitate intense selling or extensive account management. This approach kept our costs low and allowed us to deliver a valuable service. While this unique path has been instrumental in our current position, looking ahead, we recognize the importance of maintaining agency relationships and actively building our customer base to enhance our existing foundation.

Chris O'Byrne

You previously mentioned that you have worked for some big publishers. Who were some of them, and what did you did for them?

Michael

The largest one is Thompson, now Thompson Reuters, where I worked in the education division. I oversaw marketing, a call center, market research, and various marketing-related functions in my role. It proved to be an invaluable experience, and I had the privilege of learning from exceptional mentors. This period reinforced the importance of comprehending the needs of your audience.

That was relatively early in the process when I encountered a significant opportunity to understand the essence of effective marketing. We commonly lean on "market research of one," assuming that because we make purchasing decisions or navigate websites in a certain manner, everyone else must share those beliefs or behaviors. For instance, many think, *The way I buy a product is like this, so everyone else must think the same way* or *When I visit a website, the first thing I look for is X, so every website should prioritize X.*

The reality is that marketers shouldn't rely on guesswork when determining what their clients want. I understand this might seem contrary to the usual approach of marketers, but it holds true, underscoring the significance of market research. In my perspective, market research involves active engagement and doing rather than merely asking questions.

Consider the introduction of scanners at grocery stores many years ago. In that scenario, marketers swiftly discovered that people's actual behavior often differed from what they verbally expressed. Individuals might claim a preference for brand A over brand B, but when analyzing the transaction data, it revealed they consistently purchased brand B instead. This exemplifies the true power of market research; it

extends beyond simply asking potential customers about their preferences. It involves practical actions like setting up landing pages and assessing which achieves a higher conversion rate.

Actionable data holds much more value, and I believe contemporary marketers may have lost sight of this. Partly, this is due to the overwhelming volume of data available, creating the challenge of determining where to begin. Performing something as straightforward as a headline test or engaging in A/B split or multivariate testing (where different headlines, body copy, and calls to action are combined) can yield valuable insights. While computers cannot handle much of the analytical work, it remains crucial to approach these new situations with the right mindset.

How can I better understand the purchasing behavior exhibited by potential customers? I think this understanding makes all the difference. Without my background in publishing companies, I might not have fully grasped the importance of this insight. While the publishing landscape has undergone substantial changes over the years, the ultimate focus remains on providing content that captivates the audience. This explains the prevalence of clickbait headlines today, as the emphasis, unfortunately, isn't always on quality. The key lies in fostering engagement.

Chris O'Byrne

If someone wants to increase their online influence and visibility, how do they go about doing that today?

Michael

I would step back and pose a series of questions, including: "Where do you aspire to have influence?" If I'm involved in the marketing sector, targeting the luxury goods industry for influencer status might not be prudent. First, I may not possess the requisite physical appeal. Second, whether such endeavors would yield substantial benefits for myself or the audience I aim to impact remains uncertain.

The initial aspect involves identifying the addressable market and determining where you want to establish influence. Once this is clarified, we can systematically refine the strategy and the tactics required to achieve that goal. The foundational step is comprehending your objectives and identifying your addressable market.

As I often put it, the second strategy is to metaphorically "stand in front of the bus." If you want to be noticed or make an impact, you must understand the direction the metaphorical bus is heading and position yourself in its path. Attempting to alter the bus's course or persuade it to take a different route will likely be ineffective. Therefore, it's crucial to observe where the individuals you're trying to influence invest their time and focus.

The third component involves maintaining a constant presence. Some people excel at this by effectively publishing across multiple platforms. A good friend recently released a new book and dedicated much time to exploring

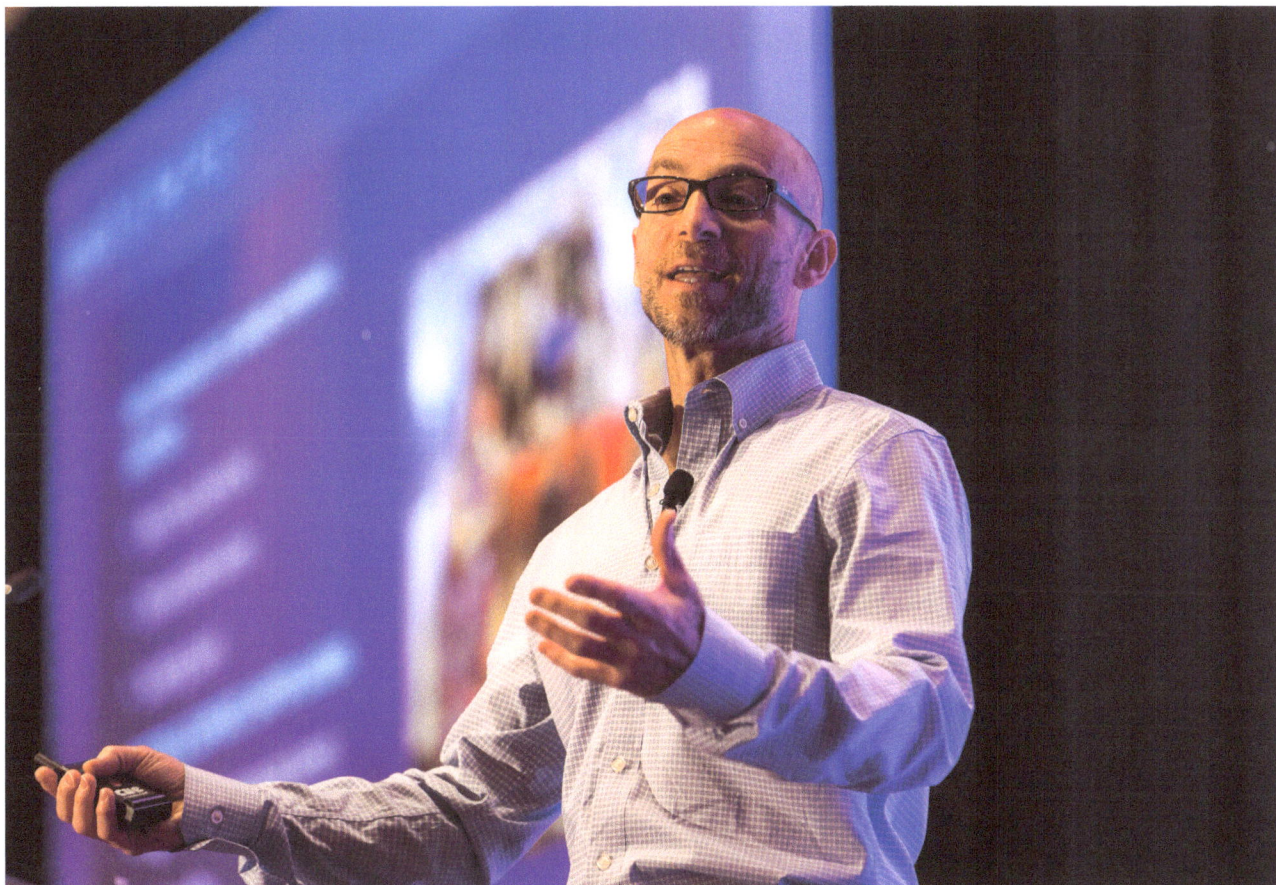

different platforms to maximize visibility.

In the end, she discovered that TikTok was the most effective platform for her. It's worth noting that, especially in the initial stages, she dedicated at least three hours daily to creating, editing, and publishing TikTok videos. Some people aren't willing to do what it takes to attain influencer status.

Eventually, she developed a huge following, with several videos going viral. This success directly resulted from the amount of time, energy, and effort she invested in the initiative. Understanding that she experimented with various approaches before discovering the one that truly resonated is vital.

She secured a book deal and successfully launched a new company thanks to the following she built. Her achievements serve as a noteworthy example. Often, people view it as an all-or-nothing scenario, expecting a single video to catapult them to millionaire status or deciding that the time and effort required are too overwhelming to attempt.

The truth lies somewhere in between. The more effort you invest, the greater the returns, with an element of luck in the mix. Returning to our initial discussion, this work revolves around defining your target audience as the addressable market. Setting realistic expectations based on what you can realistically achieve is important. Approaching it in this manner makes the process more manageable and satisfying,

aligning the level of effort with the outcomes you can attain.

Chris O'Byrne

Let's say you get your market right, know who you're influencing, and know where they are. Is the next most important thing being omnipresent, being everywhere, and having a presence on many platforms?

Michael

It needs to be approached strategically. I know someone who's been consistently posting on Instagram for as long as I can remember, yet he only has 100 followers. At some point, you must assess whether the content aligns with the audience and if the messaging is on point. To his credit, he remains persistent. Perhaps, at some point, he'll take a step back and reflect on which content garners more engagement.

Indeed, if it were easy, everyone would be doing it. Achieving influencer status, like Mr. Beast, who earns tens of millions of dollars annually, requires more than just a single video. It involves a process of creating, iterating, and learning from each attempt.

For me, the most valuable aspect lies in the process of self-discovery—understanding your strengths and weaknesses, refining your skills, becoming more adept in front of the camera, and ultimately delivering content and information that adds real value and resonates with your audience.

While quantity is essential, it's not just about quantity alone. In today's landscape, cutting through the clutter requires a balance of quality and quantity, especially given the dwindling attention spans that now hover around seven seconds. Unfortunately, having high-quality content alone is insufficient; consistent output is equally essential.

Chris O'Byrne

Who are some of the most critical influences or mentors who have helped you?

Michael

I've been fortunate to have a few mentors, and one of my early mentors, who most readers may not remember, was the former president and owner of Evelyn Wood Reading Dynamics. Evelyn Wood Reading Dynamics, founded by Evelyn Wood, was among the pioneering direct response companies. Specializing in speed, it became the first-ever speed-reading course. She sold millions of dollars of speed-reading courses through commercials, magazine ads, and direct mail. The company was later acquired by my mentor, Alan Golden, who ran it successfully for several years before selling it. Alan imparted valuable lessons to me, emphasizing the importance of practice, rehearsal, strategic thinking, showing up, and being present—life lessons that have also proved beneficial in business.

He remains a friend to this day, and we still have occasional conversations. The key is concentrating on what you want rather than what you don't want. Frequently, we harbor doubts and express concerns about things we wish to avoid, such as losing a client or facing challenges. This focus on the negative consumes a lot of attention and generates resistance to the goals you are striving to achieve.

One valuable lesson I learned from him as a mentor is the importance of always looking to the future and planning. While being present in the moment is crucial, it's equally essential to contemplate what comes next and chart the course to your desired destination. The saying holds true: If you're constantly looking in the rearview mirror, you can't drive forward.

He served as a fabulous mentor to me. Additionally, in the early stages of my career, I had the privilege of working with the CEO of the Interiors Division for USG, a Fortune 100 company (United States Gypsum Corporation). He was a very buttoned-up, wonderful guy who taught me the importance of market research. He was a thoroughly professional and insightful individual who highlighted the significance of market research. As a dedicated market research expert, we collaborated on a special project. The influence of these mentors early on taught me to do my homework and be humble throughout the process. Their guidance underscored the reality that you could be flying high one day, and the next, you could be looking for the next opportunity. I learned to respect people for their contributions and cultivate compassion for others—a lesson that originated from my early mentors.

Chris O'Byrne

What is one of the most valuable lessons you've learned?

Michael

I would argue that, at times, it can indeed be that straightforward. Often, we've been cautioned that business is inherently challenging, managing one's company is arduous, handling people is tough, and economic conditions are demanding—essentially, a barrage of negativity. Undoubtedly, these challenges are inherent in every business, a reality familiar to those who run companies.

Conversely, the flip side is also true. There are occasions when you experience some massive win, and these wins aren't always monetary. It could be the satisfaction of working with a company you genuinely admire. It might be that exceptional hire who exceeds expectations and whose accomplishments make you immensely proud, brightening your day, week, or even month.

Numerous victories far outweigh the challenges. This is the message I like to convey, especially to those who are just starting—whether as freelancers, early-career professionals, or individuals in mid-career navigating a challenging phase and contemplating a fresh start.

My advice to them is to acknowledge that things can be difficult, but remember there are also amazing, wonderful, and successful moments. It doesn't always have to be a struggle; sometimes, wins come easily. Therefore, celebrate and cherish those victories, and keep your focus on them. There's a model that illustrates two balls rolling down different paths—one follows a straight line while the other has ups and downs. Intriguingly, the one with ups and downs is faster than the straight line. This, to me, reflects the essence of business and the outlook that people should adopt. The best advice is to concentrate on the positive, celebrate your wins, and recognize that challenges are part of the overall process.

Action Steps

1. **Optimize Your Online Presence**: Utilize the insights shared by the author to assess and enhance your website's search engine optimization (SEO) and paid search strategies. This involves reviewing your current SEO tactics, updating your content with relevant keywords, and ensuring that your paid search campaigns are targeted and efficient. By doing so, you can significantly improve your visibility on search engines like Google, making it easier for potential clients or customers to find your business online.

2. **Focus on a Synergistic Marketing Approach**: Implement a combined strategy of SEO and paid search, as suggested by the author. This approach can create a more powerful and effective online marketing plan. For example, use paid search to drive immediate traffic to your site, while building your organic search ranking with SEO for long-term results. This dual strategy can help you reach a wider audience and increase your online influence.

3. **Cultivate and Manage Your Online Reputation**: Take the author's advice to heart by being proactive about your online reputation. Regularly monitor what is being said

about your business online and take steps to address any negative feedback or misinformation. Encourage satisfied customers to leave positive reviews and actively engage with your audience on social media platforms. By controlling the narrative around your brand, you can shape how you are perceived online and build trust with your audience.

About the Author

Michael Fleischner is an accomplished entrepreneur and CEO of Big Fin SEO, a search engine optimization and digital marketing agency. He is renowned for his expertise in digital marketing and as the author of SEO Made Simple and The 7-Figure Freelancer. Michael's insights have been featured on the TODAY Show, ABC World News, and Bloomberg Radio, underscoring his influence in the marketing industry.

AI IN CONTENT MARKETING: CRAFTING MESSAGES THAT RESONATE

CHRIS O'BYRNE

In today's digital era, content marketing has transcended traditional boundaries, thanks to the advent of Artificial Intelligence (AI). This transformative technology is reshaping how businesses communicate with their audience, offering unprecedented personalization and efficiency. As an entrepreneur or business leader, understanding and harnessing the power of AI in your content strategy is crucial for staying ahead. This article aims to guide you through the nuances of AI in content marketing, highlighting its benefits, implementation strategies, and ethical considerations. Embrace

AI to craft messages that not only capture attention but also resonate deeply with your audience.

Understanding AI in Content Marketing

In the realm of content marketing, Artificial Intelligence (AI) has emerged as a game-changer, transforming how businesses engage with their audiences. AI in content marketing extends beyond simple automation; it involves sophisticated algorithms that can analyze data, understand patterns, and even predict consumer behaviors. This advanced technology enables marketers to create more targeted, relevant, and personalized content, thereby elevating the user experience and increasing engagement.

The core of AI in content marketing lies in its ability to process and interpret vast amounts of data at an unprecedented speed. By leveraging natural language processing (NLP) and machine learning, AI systems can understand human language, grasp contextual nuances, and produce content that resonates with readers. This capability is not just about generating articles or social media posts. It's about creating a narrative that aligns with the interests, needs, and preferences of the target audience.

Moreover, AI's role in content marketing is not limited to content creation. It extends to content curation and distribution as well. AI tools can analyze the performance of various content pieces across different channels and suggest optimal distribution strategies. This ensures that the right content reaches the right audience at the right time, maximizing impact and engagement.

Another significant aspect of AI in content marketing is its predictive analytics feature. By analyzing past consumer behavior and market trends, AI can forecast future patterns and preferences. This foresight allows marketers to stay ahead of the curve, crafting content strategies that align with anticipated changes in consumer behavior.

However, the integration of AI in content marketing also demands a strategic approach. It's essential for marketers to understand the capabilities and limitations of AI tools and to use them in ways that complement human creativity and insight. While AI can generate data-driven content, the human touch in storytelling and understanding audience sentiment remains irreplaceable.

Understanding AI in content marketing is about recognizing its potential to transform traditional marketing strategies. It offers a blend of efficiency, personalization, and predictive power, making it an invaluable asset for any marketer. As AI technology continues to evolve, its role in content marketing is set to become more prominent, offering exciting opportunities for innovation and engagement.

Benefits of AI in Content Marketing

The integration of Artificial Intelligence (AI) in content marketing brings a multitude of benefits that revolutionize how businesses connect with their audience. One of the most significant advantages is the ability to personalize content at scale. AI algorithms can analyze individual user data and preferences, enabling the creation of highly tailored content. This personalized approach ensures that each piece of content speaks directly to the needs and interests of each segment of the audience, thereby increasing engagement and loyalty.

Efficiency and scalability are other notable benefits of AI in content marketing. Traditional content creation processes can be time-consuming and often hit limits in terms of scale. AI, however, can generate content quickly and efficiently, handling the heavy lifting of content production. This frees up human marketers to focus on more creative and strategic aspects of content marketing. Additionally, AI can manage and optimize content distribution across various channels, ensuring that content reaches the widest possible audience in the most effective manner.

Data-driven insights stand as another crucial advantage. AI tools can sift through vast amounts of data to extract meaningful insights about consumer behavior and market trends. These insights enable marketers to make informed decisions about content strategy, from what topics to cover to how to frame messages for maximum impact. This data-centric approach ensures that content marketing efforts are grounded in actual consumer needs and

preferences, leading to higher engagement and conversion rates.

AI also enhances creativity in content marketing. Contrary to the belief that AI might stifle human creativity, it actually provides new opportunities for creative expression. AI can suggest novel content ideas, formats, and angles that might not be immediately apparent to human marketers. It can also assist in creating visually appealing designs and layouts for content, making it more engaging and shareable.

Lastly, AI in content marketing offers improved ROI tracking and analytics. AI-powered analytics tools provide a deeper understanding of content performance, enabling marketers to measure the impact of their content more accurately and make data-driven adjustments to their strategies.

The benefits of AI in content marketing are transformative. From personalization to enhanced efficiency, data-driven insights, creative augmentation, and improved analytics, AI empowers marketers to create more impactful, relevant, and successful content strategies. As the digital landscape continues to evolve, AI in content marketing is not just an advantage; it's becoming an essential component of a successful digital marketing strategy.

Implementing AI in Your Content Strategy

Implementing AI in your content strategy is a journey that begins with understanding your current marketing capabilities and determining how AI can enhance them. The first step involves assessing your existing content marketing approach to identify areas where AI can add value. This might include automating repetitive tasks, personalizing content for different audience segments, or analyzing large sets of data for insights.

Once the areas of potential AI application are identified, the next step is integrating AI tools into your existing content strategy. This involves choosing the right AI tools that align with your specific needs. The market offers a wide range of AI solutions for content creation, curation, optimization, and analytics. Selecting the right tools requires a clear understanding of your marketing goals and the capabilities of different AI technologies.

Training and resources are critical in this implementation phase. AI tools, while powerful, have a learning curve, and it's vital that your team is adequately trained to use them effectively. This might involve formal training sessions, hiring new talent with AI expertise, or collaborating with AI service providers for support and guidance.

Another key aspect of implementing AI in your content strategy is data management. AI systems require access to high-quality data to function effectively. Ensuring that your data is clean, organized, and accessible is crucial. This might involve setting up data collection and management systems that are compatible with your chosen AI tools.

Once AI tools are integrated into your content strategy, continuous monitoring and optimization are essential. AI-driven content strategies should be dynamic, with regular adjustments based on performance metrics and changing market trends. This involves regularly reviewing the outputs of AI tools and ensuring they align with your overall content marketing goals.

Finally, it's important to maintain a balance between AI-driven content and human creativity. AI can provide valuable insights and automate certain tasks, but the human element in content creation and strategy is irreplaceable. The most successful content strategies use AI as a tool to enhance, rather than replace, human creativity and intuition.

Implementing AI in your content strategy is a multi-faceted process that involves assessment, integration, training, data management, continuous monitoring, and balancing AI with human input. By carefully navigating these steps, businesses can effectively harness the power of AI to enhance their content marketing efforts and achieve greater success in their digital marketing endeavors.

Ethical Considerations and Best Practices

Incorporating AI into content marketing raises important ethical considerations that must be addressed to maintain trust and authenticity. The first of these is the ethical use of data. AI systems rely heavily on data to generate content and insights, making it imperative to handle consumer data responsibly. Ensuring data privacy, obtaining proper consent for data usage, and being transparent about how data is used are essential steps in maintaining ethical standards.

Another key consideration is the authenticity of AI-generated content. While AI can produce content efficiently, it's crucial to ensure that this content remains true to your brand's voice and values. The goal is to use AI as a tool to enhance content quality without compromising the authenticity that builds trust with your audience.

Transparency is also vital when using AI in content marketing. This involves being open about the use of AI in content creation and curation processes. Audiences value honesty, and being upfront about the use of AI helps maintain a trustful relationship with your audience.

In terms of best practices, maintaining a balance between AI and human input is paramount. While AI can automate and optimize many aspects of content marketing, the human touch is irreplaceable in understanding audience nuances and maintaining the brand's essence. Regularly reviewing AI-generated content and tweaking it as necessary ensures it aligns with your brand's tone and style.

Quality control is another best practice that cannot be overlooked. Regularly auditing AI-generated content for accuracy, relevance, and quality ensures that the content meets your standards and resonates with your audience. This includes checking for errors that AI might overlook and ensuring that the content is contextually appropriate.

Lastly, staying updated with AI developments and ethical guidelines is crucial. The field of AI is rapidly evolving, and staying informed about new tools, techniques, and ethical considerations is important to use AI responsibly and effectively in content marketing.

The ethical considerations and best practices in using AI for content marketing revolve around responsible data use, maintaining authenticity, transparency, balancing AI with human input, quality control, and staying informed about AI advancements. By adhering to these principles, businesses can leverage AI in content marketing effectively while maintaining ethical standards and building trust with their audience.

Conclusion

As we have explored, AI stands as a pivotal tool in revolutionizing content marketing strategies. It offers a unique blend of personalization, efficiency, and creative enhancement, empowering businesses to connect with their audience more effectively. While embracing AI, remember to balance innovation with ethical considerations and maintain your brand's authenticity. The future of content marketing is bright and AI-driven; by integrating these intelligent solutions into your strategy, you can create compelling, resonant content that elevates your brand and engages your audience like never before. The journey into AI-enhanced content marketing is not just an option; it's a strategic imperative for success.

Action Steps

- Evaluate and Identify AI Opportunities

    Start by conducting a thorough evaluation of your current content marketing strategy. Identify areas where AI can bring significant improvements, such as content personalization, data analysis, or process automation. This step involves understanding your audience's needs and how AI can help meet them more effectively. Use this evaluation to set clear objectives for incorporating AI into your strategy, such as increasing audience engagement, improving content relevance, or streamlining content production.

- Invest in Suitable AI Tools and Training

    Once you've identified how AI can enhance your content marketing, the next step is to invest in the right AI tools. Choose tools that align with your specific needs and objectives identified in Step 1. This might include AI platforms for content creation, analytics tools for audience insights, or automation tools for content distribution. Equally important is investing in training for yourself and your team. Ensure everyone involved understands how to use these tools effectively. This may involve attending workshops, webinars, or hiring a consultant to provide in-depth training on AI applications in content marketing.

- Implement, Monitor, and Refine

    With the right tools and training in place, begin implementing AI in your content marketing strategy. Start with small, manageable projects to gauge the effectiveness of AI in your processes. Monitor the performance of AI-driven content closely, using analytics to understand its impact on your audience engagement and marketing goals. Be prepared to refine and adjust your strategy based on these insights. Regularly review and update your AI applications to ensure they continue to meet your evolving content marketing needs and remain aligned with industry best practices and ethical standards.

www.ingramcontent.com/pod-product-compliance
Lightning Source LLC
Chambersburg PA
CBHW052052190326

41519CB00002BA/193